AQA GCSE (9–1) Foundation

Combined Science Trilogy and Entry Level Certificate Workbook

Gemma Young
Alan Denton
Jeremy Pollard
Nigel Saunders
Catherine Wilson

Collins

William Collins' dream of knowledge for all began with the publication of his first book in 1819.

A self-educated mill worker, he not only enriched millions of lives, but also founded a flourishing publishing house. Today, staying true to this spirit, Collins books are packed with inspiration, innovation and practical expertise. They place you at the centre of a world of possibility and give you exactly what you need to explore it.

Collins. Freedom to teach.

Published by Collins
An imprint of HarperCollins*Publishers*
The News Building
1 London Bridge Street
London
SE1 9GF

Browse the complete Collins catalogue at
www.collins.co.uk

10 9 8 7 6

ISBN 978-0-00-833502-1

British Library Cataloguing in Publication Data
A catalogue record for this publication is available from the British Library.

Authors: Gemma Young, Alan Denton, Jeremy Pollard, Nigel Saunders, Catherine Wilson
Publisher: Katie Sergeant
In-house editor: Joanna Ramsay
Development editor: Jane Glendening
Copyeditor: Peter Batty
Proofreader: David Hemsley
Cover designer: The Big Mountain Design
Typesetter: Jouve India Ltd
Production controller: Katharine Willard
Printed and bound by: Ashford Colour Press Ltd

Cover(t) Respiro/Shutterstock, Cover(b) Tschub/Shutterstock, pp4-5 Guenter Albers/Shutterstock, p9 plenoy m/Shutterstock, p22 Crystal Eye Studio/Shutterstock, p24 areeya_ann/Shutterstock, p28 Soleil Nordic/Shutterstock, p32 AntonZzz/Shutterstock, p39 Sujichin/Shutterstock, p43 jagoda/Shutterstock, p45 IanRedding/Shutterstock, p46 Kazakova Maryia/Shutterstock, p47 garanga/Shutterstock, p49(t) Marek Trawczynski/Shutterstock, p50 Svetlana Foote/Shutterstock,, pp54-55 Sebastian Janicki/Shutterstock, p57 bonchan/Shutterstock, p59 Andrew Lambert/Science Photo Library, p61 Andrey_Popov/Shutterstock, p63(t) ElRoi/Shutterstock, p63(b) beeboys/Shutterstock, p69 RennieRST/Shutterstock, p71 Nigel Wallace/Shutterstock, p75 hiv360/Shutterstock, p92 moj0j0/Shutterstock, pp104-105 ShutterStockStudio/Shutterstock, p107 bunnyphoto/Shutterstock, p108 Lukas Gojda/Shutterstock, p112 abutyrin/Shutterstock, p115(t) Caracarafoto/Shutterstock, p115(b) BlueRingMedia/, Shutterstock, p116 Byron Palmer/Shutterstock, p117 Sari ONeal/Shutterstock, p123(l) juliasv/Shutterstock, p123(r) Timmary/, Shutterstock, p124(t) Friedrich Saurer/Science Photo Library, p126 Victor Moussa/Shutterstock, p127 urfin/Shutterstock, p134 ludinko/Shutterstock, p135(t) Caron Badkin/Shutterstock, p135(b) Andrey Snegirev/Shutterstock, p136(l) Hurst Photo/Shutterstock, p136(m) sutsaiy/Shutterstock, p136(r) You can more/Shutterstock, p137 ppart/Shutterstock, p141 Spencer Grant/Science Photo Library, p143 Designua/Shutterstock, p149 Mr.Exen/Shutterstock, p151(tl) Jiang Hongyan/Shutterstock, p151(tr) sutsaiy/Shutterstock, p156(b) garanga/Shutterstock, p157 Fancy Tapis/Shutterstock, p159(t) Neamov/Shutterstock, p159(bl) xpixel/Shutterstock, p159(br) Fablok/Shutterstock, p160(b) Huguette Roe/Shutterstock, p161 Joy Brown/Shutterstock.

HarperCollins*Publishers*
Macken House
39/40 Mayor Street Upper
Dublin 1
DO1 C9W8
Ireland

The publishers gratefully acknowledge the permission granted to reproduce the copyright material in this book. Every effort has been made to trace copyright holders and to obtain their permission for the use of copyright material. The publishers will gladly receive any information enabling them to rectify any error or omission at the first opportunity.

Contents

Introduction

Build your confidence for the AQA Entry Level Certificate, Combined Science Trilogy or Synergy course.

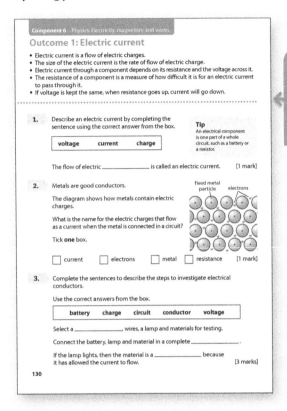

Remind yourself of the key information with a summary for each outcome.

Test your knowledge and understanding with questions for each outcome.

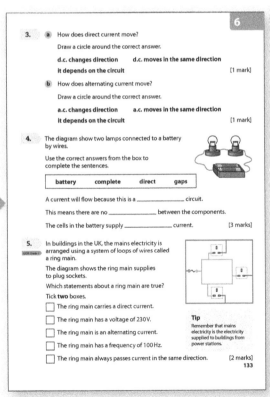

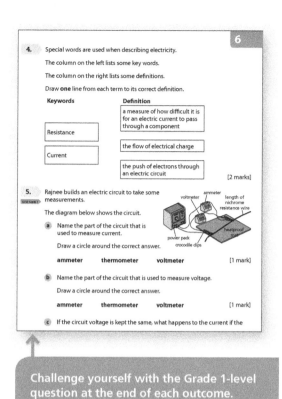

4. Special words are used when describing electricity.

The column on the left lists some key words.

The column on the right lists some definitions.

Draw **one** line from each term to its correct definition.

Keywords   **Definition**

a measure of how difficult it is for an electric current to pass through a component

Resistance

the flow of electrical charge

Current

the push of electrons through an electric circuit

[2 marks]

5. Rajnee builds an electric circuit to take some measurements.

The diagram below shows the circuit.

a Name the part of the circuit that is used to measure current.

Draw a circle around the correct answer.

ammeter   thermometer   voltmeter   [1 mark]

b Name the part of the circuit that is used to measure voltage.

Draw a circle around the correct answer.

ammeter   thermometer   voltmeter   [1 mark]

c If the circuit voltage is kept the same, what happens to the current if the

Challenge yourself with the Grade 1-level question at the end of each outcome.

Glossary
Biology

Abiotic: Non-living factor of an ecosystem.

Absorbed: Or 'taken in': useful products from digestion are absorbed through the wall of the intestine into the blood.

Acid rain: When sulfur dioxide and other gases such as oxides of nitrogen dissolve in rain water an acidic solution known as 'acid rain' is formed.

Action: Any response which our body carries out, such as kicking, walking or blinking.

Adapted: An adapted organism has characteristics to suit the conditions where it lives. For example, a polar bear has thick, white fur.

Addictive: An addictive substance is one that your body becomes dependent on: once you start taking it, you want more and it is difficult to give up.

Algae: Organisms previously thought of as plants. Algae have chlorophyll but lack true stems, roots, and leaves.

Antibiotic: A drug that acts on bacteria.

Antibody: A substance produced by the body to fight disease. Antibodies are proteins that are produced by the immune system.

Asexual reproduction: A way of reproducing new identical offspring from only one parent.

Automatic: A response happens without thinking about it; we cannot control automatic reactions.

Bacteria: Simple microscopic single-celled organisms; some are good for the body, others can cause illness and disease.

Biotic: Living components that affect population size or the environment such as predators.

Blood: A fluid that our heart pumps around our whole body.

Brain: A large organ inside the skull; it receives and processes information from body sensors and uses this information to make decisions.

Carbon cycle: How carbon is recycled so that it can be used again.

Carbon dioxide: a gas produced by burning fossil fuels and by respiration.

cytoplasm   cell membrane

nucleus

Cell Membrane: Surrounds the cell and controls movement of substances in and out.

Characteristics: The features that distinguish one person from another, for example the shape of nose or colour of eyes.

Chlorophyll: The green pigment in plants and algae, which absorbs light energy.

Chromosomes: The thread-like structures containing tightly coiled DNA.

Clone: An organism that is genetically identical to another organism.

Competition: When two or more living things struggle against each other to get the same resource.

Consumer: Feeds on another organism.

Contraceptive: A method designed to prevent the fertilisation of an egg.

Coordinated: If processes are coordinated it means that they are working together for the same purpose.

Cutting: A piece of a plant (often a leaf) that is cut off; it can then be planted in soil to grow a new plant.

Check the meaning of the key words in the glossary.

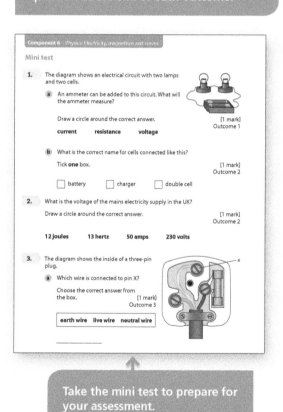

Component 6 Physics: Electricity, magnetism and waves

Mini test

1. The diagram shows an electrical circuit with two lamps and two cells.

a An ammeter can be added to this circuit. What will the ammeter measure?

Draw a circle around the correct answer.   [1 mark]
Outcome 1

current   resistance   voltage

b What is the correct name for cells connected like this?

Tick **one** box.   [1 mark]
Outcome 2

☐ battery   ☐ charger   ☐ double cell

2. What is the voltage of the mains electricity supply in the UK?

Draw a circle around the correct answer.   [1 mark]
Outcome 2

12 joules   13 hertz   50 amps   230 volts

3. The diagram shows the inside of a three-pin plug.

a Which wire is connected to pin X?

Choose the correct answer from the box.   [1 mark]
Outcome 3

earth wire   live wire   neutral wire

_____

Take the mini test to prepare for your assessment.

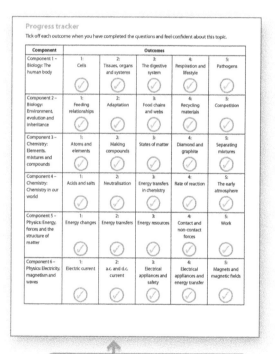

Progress tracker

Tick off each outcome when you have completed the questions and feel confident about this topic.

Component	Outcomes				
Component 1 – Biology: The human body	1: Cells ✓	2: Tissues, organs and systems ✓	3: The digestive system ✓	4: Respiration and lifestyle ✓	5: Pathogens ✓
Component 2 – Biology: Environment, evolution and inheritance	1: Feeding relationships ✓	2: Adaptation ✓	3: Food chains and webs ✓	4: Recycling materials ✓	5: Competition ✓
Component 3 – Chemistry: Elements, mixtures and compounds	1: Atoms and elements ✓	2: Making compounds ✓	3: States of matter ✓	4: Diamond and graphite ✓	5: Separating mixtures ✓
Component 4 – Chemistry: Chemistry in our world	1: Acids and salts ✓	2: Neutralisation ✓	3: Energy transfers in chemistry ✓	4: Rate of reaction ✓	5: The early atmosphere ✓
Component 5 – Physics: Energy, forces and the structure of matter	1: Energy changes ✓	2: Energy transfers ✓	3: Energy resources ✓	4: Contact and non-contact forces ✓	5: Work ✓
Component 6 – Physics: Electricity, magnetism and waves	1: Electric current ✓	2: a.c. and d.c. current ✓	3: Electrical appliances and safety ✓	4: Electrical appliances and energy transfer ✓	5: Magnets and magnetic fields ✓

Tick off each outcome once you feel confident on that topic.

There are answers to all the questions at the back of the book. You can check your answers yourself or your teacher might tear them out and give them to you later to help you mark your work.

Outcome 1: Cells

- Plants and animals are composed of cells.
- Animal cells have three main parts: the cell membrane, cytoplasm and nucleus.
- Cells are specialised. They have special features, so they can carry out a function.

1. Use the correct answers from the box to label the diagram of a human cell.

| cell membrane | cytoplasm | nucleus | platelet |

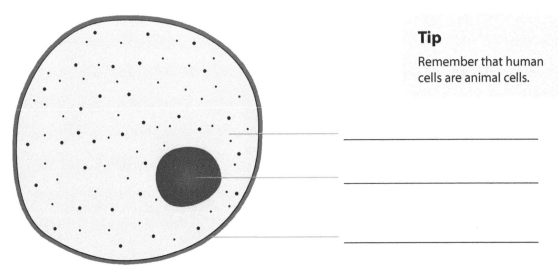

Tip

Remember that human cells are animal cells.

[3 marks]

2. Each cell part has a different function.

The column on the left lists parts of a cell.

The column on the right lists the function of the parts.

Draw **one** line from each part to its function.

Part

Function

Part	Function
Nucleus	contains genetic information, which controls the activities of the cell
Cytoplasm	controls what enters and leaves the cell
Cell membrane	where chemical reactions happen

[3 marks]

3. Cells in the human body are specialised to carry out different functions.

This means that they are different shapes and sizes according to their function.

Use the correct answers from the box to complete each sentence.

blood	egg	muscle	nerve	sperm

Nerve impulses are carried around the body by _____ cells.

The _____ cell joins with the male sex cell.

The heart can change shape because it contains _____ cells.

[3 marks]

4. The picture shows a cell.

tail ————

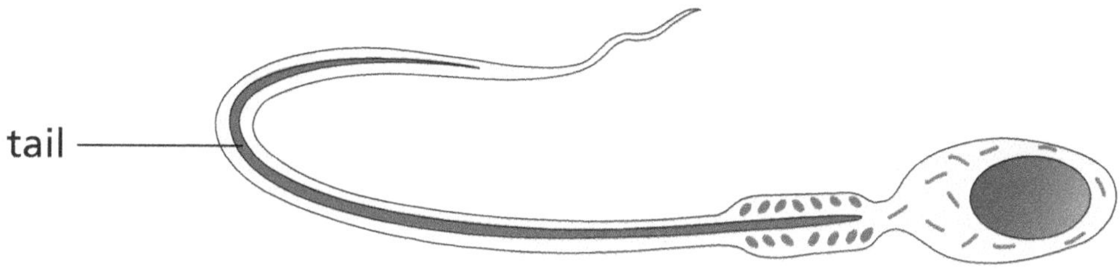

a Name the cell.

_____

[1 mark]

b Describe how its tail helps the cell to carry out its function.

_____

_____

_____ [2 marks]

Outcome 2: Tissues, organs and systems

- Specialised cells are grouped together to form tissues.
- Organs are made up of different tissues working together to carry out a function.
- Organs work together in systems.

1.   Write these structures into the correct boxes below, to show the correct order in size.

organ   tissue   cell

smallest [ ] ➡ [ ] ➡ [ ] **largest**   [1 mark]

2.   Organs have a function in the body.

The column on the left lists some organs.

The column on the right lists the function of organs.

Draw **one** line from each part to its function.

Organ	**Function of organ**
Brain	filters the blood and produces urine (a liquid waste)
Kidney	does many jobs, including removing toxins from the blood
Liver	receives and processes information

[3 marks]

3.   Which organs are reproductive organs?

Tick **two** boxes.

[ ]   kidneys

[ ]   testes

[ ]   lungs

[ ]   ovaries

[2 marks]

4. The human circulatory system contains the heart, which pumps blood around the body.

Write numbers 1–4 in the boxes to show the order of events that happen.

The first one has been done to help you.

Blood is pumped around the body	

In the lungs carbon dioxide leaves the blood and oxygen enters it	

Blood high in oxygen enters the heart	1

Blood high in carbon dioxide returns to the heart and is pumped to the lungs	

[3 marks]

5. The photograph is a magnified image of blood.

It shows red and white blood cells.

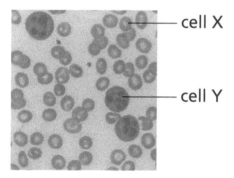
cell X

cell Y

Complete the table.

Tip
The photograph is pink because a stain is used so that the cells can be seen more clearly.

Cell	Name	Function
X		
Y		

[4 marks]

Outcome 3: The digestive system

- The human digestive system contains several organs: salivary glands, oesophagus (gullet), stomach, liver, gall bladder, pancreas, small intestine, large intestine.
- Enzymes are used to help break down food into soluble substances that can be absorbed into the blood.

1. Use the correct answers from the box to label the organs of the digestive system.

large intestine   liver   oesophagus   pancreas   small intestine   stomach

[4 marks]

2. Which organs does food pass through?

Tick **two** boxes.

☐ stomach   ☐ gall bladder

☐ salivary glands   ☐ small intestine   [2 marks]

3. Which sentence best describes digestion?

Tick **one** box.

☐ The process of breaking down food into simple substances that the blood can absorb.

☐ The process of breaking up large pieces of food into smaller ones that can be swallowed.

☐ The process of moving food through the digestive system.   [1 mark]

4. The organs in the digestive system each have a function.

Use the correct answers from the box to complete each sentence.

liver	mouth	pancreas	small intestine	stomach

Acidic juices in the _____ start the digestion of protein and kill microorganisms.

The _____ is a gland that releases enzymes into the small intestine.

Enzymes help break down food into soluble substances that are absorbed into

the blood through the walls of the _____ .   [3 marks]

5. Amylase is an enzyme that helps break down a substance called starch.

GCSE Grade 1

Manvir and Jessica investigate the effect of amylase on starch.

They follow this method:

1. Add amylase to a test tube containing starch solution.

2. Every 30 seconds take some of the mixture from the test tube and add to iodine.

If the mixture contains starch the iodine goes black.

If the mixture does not contain starch the iodine will stay orange.

a Describe how they will know when all the starch had been broken down.

_____ [1 mark]

b They decide to increase the volume of amylase. They kept the volume of starch the same.

Complete the prediction.

I think that the time taken for starch to be

broken down will _____ .

Tip

Say if you think the time will increase or decrease.

I think this because:

_____ [2 marks]

Outcome 4: Respiration and lifestyle

- Respiration takes place in cells. Energy needed for living processes is released when glucose and oxygen react.
- Lifestyle can affect the health of a person.
- A healthy diet contains the right balance of the different foods you need and the right amount of energy.
- People who exercise regularly are usually fitter than people who take little exercise.

1. Respiration is a chemical reaction. It releases energy.

   a Use the correct answers from the box to complete the word equation for respiration.

air	oxygen	starch	water

   glucose + _____ → carbon + dioxide _____ (+ energy)   [2 marks]

   b Glucose is needed for respiration.

   Where do we get glucose from?

   _____   [1 mark]

   Tip
   Energy is in brackets because it is released during the reaction, but it is not a substance.

   c Carbon dioxide is made during respiration.

   Where in the body is carbon dioxide removed from the blood?

   _____   [1 mark]

2. Lifestyle can affect a person's health.

   The column on the left lists some lifestyle choices.

   The column on the right lists the effect on a person's health.

   Draw **one** line from each lifestyle choice to its effect.

   Lifestyle choice

Smoking

Drinking too much alcohol

   Effect on health

liver and brain damage

lung cancer

   [2 marks]

3. Bryony and Isabel go for a run.

They draw a graph to show how their pulse rate changed.

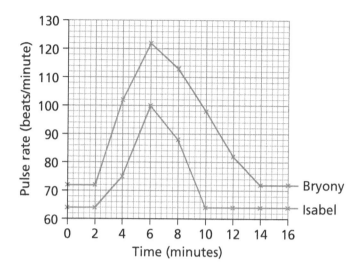

They started to run after 2 minutes.

How does the graph show this?

_____ [1 mark]

4. Look at the graph in question 3.

GCSE Grade 1

a Who is fitter – Bryony or Isabel? _____ [1 mark]

b Describe how you can you tell this from the graph.

_____ [1 mark]

Outcome 5: Pathogens

- Microorganisms called pathogens cause infectious (communicable) diseases.
- Bacteria may reproduce quickly inside the body and may produce poisons (toxins) that make us feel ill.
- Viruses reproduce inside cells, which damages the cells.

1. Measles is an infectious disease caused by a virus.

   What is an infectious disease?

   _____ [1 mark]

2. Which disease is **not** infectious?

   Tick **one** box.

   ☐ common cold

   ☐ cancer

   ☐ flu

   ☐ chickenpox

   Tip
   Infectious diseases are diseases that can be passed from person to person.

   [1 mark]

3. Ruby is not feeling well. She has developed a disease caused by bacteria.

   Use the correct answers from the box to complete each sentence.

die	diseases	reproduce	toxins	viruses

   The bacteria _____ quickly inside her body.

   The bacteria produce _____ which make her feel ill.   [2 marks]

4. Max measures his temperature every morning for 10 days.

On day 2 he becomes infected with bacteria.

He draws a graph.

a What is his normal body temperature?

_____ °C [1 mark]

b He felt ill on days 5–7.

What happened to his body temperature on these days?

_____ [1 mark]

5. Not all bacteria cause disease.

GCSE Grade 1

a What is the difference in effects on the human body between bacteria that cause disease and ones that do not?

_____

_____ [2 marks]

b Most viruses cause disease.

Explain why.

_____

_____ [2 marks]

Outcome 6: Fighting disease

- White blood cells ingest (consume) bacteria and produce antibodies.
- During vaccination dead or inactive forms of a pathogen are placed into the body.
- Vaccination stimulates the white blood cells to produce antibodies so that if the same pathogen re-enters the body, antibodies can be produced quickly.

1. White blood cells help the body to fight disease.

   Which is a substance they produce to do this?

   Tick **one** box.

   ☐ vaccines   ☐ antibodies

   ☐ toxins   ☐ pathogens   [1 mark]

2. The diagram shows a human cell about to attack a group of pathogens.

   a Use the correct answers from the box to label the diagram.

   | bacteria   red blood cell   white blood cell |

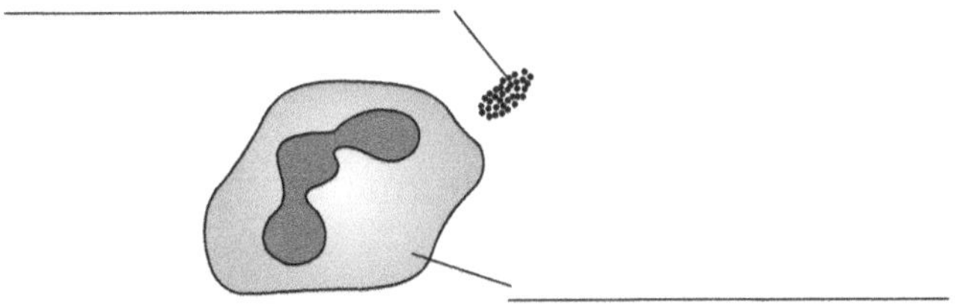

   [2 marks]

   b Describe how the cell destroys the pathogens.

   _____ [1 mark]

3. Connor has a measles vaccination.

   a What is injected into his body during the vaccination?

   Tick **one** box.

   ☐ a live virus   ☐ an inactive virus

   ☐ a white blood cell   ☐ an antibody   [1 mark]

b Write the numbers 1–3 in the boxes to show the order of what happens after Connor is vaccinated.

| White blood cells start to produce antibodies to fight the virus. | ☐ |

| If Connor becomes infected with active measles viruses his body will quickly produce antibodies. | ☐ |

| The white blood cells remember how to make the antibodies for the measles virus. | ☐ | [3 marks]

c Why does the vaccination not give Connor measles?

_____ [1 mark]

d A few months after the vaccination, measles viruses enter Connor's body.

Why does he not get ill?

_____

_____ [2 marks]

4. In 1968 people started getting the measles vaccination in the UK.

GCSE Grade 1

The table shows how many people got measles in England and Wales.

Year	Number of people who got measles
1970	307 408
1980	139 487
1990	13 302
2000	2378
2010	2235

a How did the number of people getting measles change after the vaccination was used?

_____ [1 mark]

b Give a reason for this.

_____ [1 mark]

Outcome 7: Drugs

- Drugs change the chemical processes in people's bodies.
- Drugs used as medicine are developed and tested by scientists before being used.
- People may become addicted to drugs and have withdrawal symptoms without them.
- Antibiotics are medicines that kill harmful bacteria inside the body.

1. Drugs change chemical processes in the body.

   Which substance is a drug?

   Tick **one** box.

   ☐ sugar   ☐ water

   ☐ oxygen   ☐ alcohol   [1 mark]

2. Antibiotics are types of drugs that can help cure diseases.

   a Which drug is an antibiotic?

   Tick **one** box.

   ☐ paracetamol   ☐ ibuprofen

   ☐ penicillin   ☐ aspirin   [1 mark]

   b Shabnam has a cold.

   Colds are caused by viruses.

   Taking an antibiotic will not cure her cold. Why not?

   _____   [1 mark]

3. Nicotine is a drug found in tobacco.

   Complete the sentences.

   Once a person starts smoking tobacco it may be difficult to stop. This is

   because nicotine is _____ .

   If they give up smoking they may suffer from unpleasant effects

   called _____ symptoms.   [2 marks]

4. Some drugs are medicines.

Why do new medicines have to be tested before they are used?

Tick **two** boxes.

☐ To check that the medicine is safe.

☐ To check the cost of the medicine.

☐ To check that the medicine works.

☐ To check that the medicine is legal. [2 marks]

5. Maryam and Ben investigated the effect of two different antibiotics on bacteria.

GCSE Grade 1

They spread bacteria onto two dishes of agar jelly.

Next, they place a small disc of paper containing the antibiotics in the centre of each dish.

The diagram shows the dishes after 24 hours.

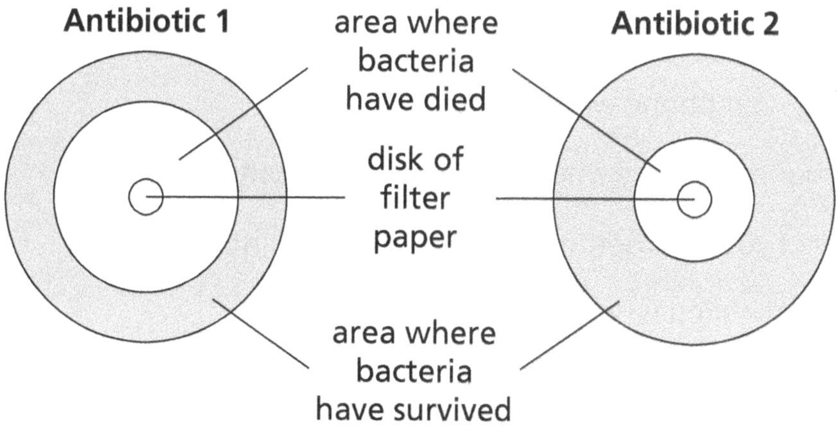

Which antibiotic is the most effective?

_____

How can you tell from the diagram?

_____

_____ [2 marks]

Tip
The antibiotic will spread through the agar jelly

Outcome 8: Control systems

- Responses in the body can be coordinated by the nervous system or hormones.
- Reflex actions are responses that are automatic and very fast.

1. The nervous system coordinates responses.

What parts of the body are part of the nervous system?

Tick **two** boxes.

☐ brain   ☐ heart

☐ nerve cells   ☐ white blood cells   [2 marks]

2. When something is about to go into your eyes you blink.

This is a reflex action.

Which other responses are reflex actions?

Tick **two** boxes.

> **Tip**
> You carry out a reflex action without thinking about it.

☐ Answering your phone when it rings.

☐ Pulling your hand away when you touch a hot pan.

☐ The pupil of your eye getting smaller in bright light.

☐ Turning on the light when you enter a dark room.   [2 marks]

3. Reflex actions help protect us from danger.

Use the correct answers from the box to complete each sentence.

automatic	fast	slow	voluntary

The speed of reflex actions is very _____ .

They happen without us thinking about them. This means

they are _____ .   [2 marks]

4. Charlie and Megan use a smartphone to investigate their reaction times.

A green box appears on the screen.

As soon as the box turns red, they touch it.

The time taken for them to touch the box is measured in seconds.

They repeat this twice.

The table shows their times.

	Time taken to touch the box in seconds		
	Turn 1	Turn 2	Mean
Charlie	0.21	0.23	0.22
Megan	0.24	0.20	

Charlie's mean is found by doing this calculation:

$$\text{Mean} = \frac{0.21 + 0.23}{2} = \frac{0.44}{2} = 0.22$$

a Calculate Megan's mean time.

_____ seconds   [1 mark]

b Charlie wants to know if drinking coffee increases his reaction time.

How could he find out?

_____

_____ [2 marks]

Outcome 9: Hormones

- Hormones are chemicals that act as 'messengers' around the body.
- They are secreted (released) by glands and are transported in the blood to their target organs.
- Several hormones are involved in the menstrual cycle of a woman.

1. Insulin is a hormone secreted from the pancreas.

It causes the liver to take up glucose from the blood.

Use the correct answers from the box to complete the sentences.

blood	gland	hormone	liver	pancreas

The pancreas is a _____ .

The target organ for insulin is the _____ .

Insulin travels to its target organ in the _____ .   [3 marks]

2. The menstrual cycle is a series of changes that happen in a woman's body.

The diagram shows the menstrual cycle.

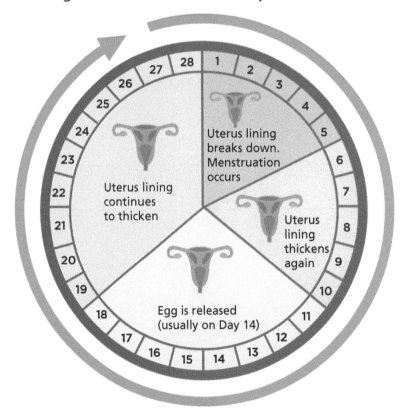

27 28 1 2 3 4 5 6 7 8 9 10 11 12 13 14 15 16 17 18 19 20 21 22 23 24 25 26

Uterus lining breaks down. Menstruation occurs

Uterus lining thickens again

Uterus lining continues to thicken

Egg is released (usually on Day 14)

a How many days does the menstrual cycle last? _____ [1 mark]

b What day in the cycle does menstruation start? _____ [1 mark]

3. The hormones oestrogen and progesterone are involved in the menstrual cycle.

The graph shows how levels of them change during the menstrual cycle.

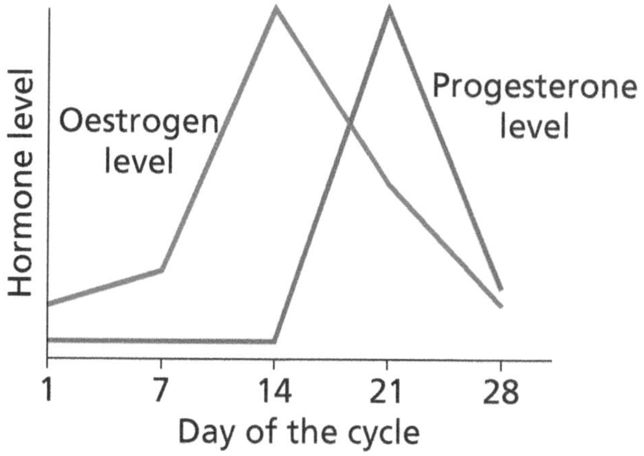

a Complete the sentences.

Oestrogen is highest on day _____ .

Progesterone is highest on day _____ . [2 marks]

b Which hormone causes the egg to be released? How does the graph show this?

_____

_____ [2 marks]

4. A woman wants to get pregnant.

GCSE Grade 1

Which days in her menstrual cycle should she have sex on?

Tick **one** box.

☐ days 1–5

☐ days 6–10

☐ days 11–18

☐ days 19–28

Tip
For her to get pregnant, sperm has to meet an egg

[1 mark]

Outcome 10: Controlling fertility

- Hormones are used to control fertility.
- Oral contraceptives contain hormones to stop eggs from maturing (growing to full size).
- Fertility drugs stimulate eggs so that they mature.

1. Karen is infertile.

What could cause this?

Tick **two** boxes.

Tip

If a woman is fertile it means she can produce a baby.

☐ She only releases one egg in each menstrual cycle.

☐ She does not release any eggs.

☐ Her eggs do not mature.

☐ She takes fertility drugs.   [2 marks]

2. Taking an oral contraceptive prevents pregnancy.

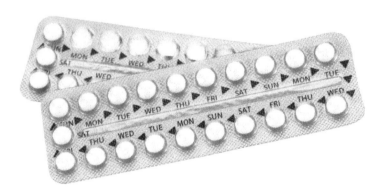

Use the correct answers from the box to complete each sentence.

inhibit	injection	pill	stimulate

Oral contraceptives are taken as a _____ .

They contain hormones that _____ eggs from maturing.   [2 marks]

3. There are advantages and disadvantages to taking an oral contraceptive.

a Which is an advantage?

Tick **one** box.

☐ They are 99% effective at preventing pregnancy.

☐ They have to be prescribed by a doctor.

☐ They can increase blood pressure.

☐ They may cause weight gain. [1 mark]

b For oral contraceptives to be effective they have to be taken every day.

Why is this a disadvantage?

_____ [1 mark]

4. Fertility drugs stimulate eggs to mature.

GCSE Grade 1

a How do fertility drugs help a woman to become pregnant?

_____

_____ [2 marks]

b Fertility drugs can cause multiple eggs to be released at once.

Why is this a disadvantage?

_____

_____ [2 marks]

Mini test

1. Respiration releases energy.

Which substance needed for respiration comes from the air?

Tick **one** box. [1 mark]
Outcome 4

☐ carbon dioxide

☐ oxygen

☐ water

2. The human body contains organ systems.

a Use the correct answers from the box to complete each sentence. [2 marks]
Outcome 2

membranes	muscles	organs	tissues

Specialised cells group together to form _____ .

Different types working together to carry out a function form

_____ .

These work together in systems.

b The column on the left lists organ systems.

The column on the right lists their functions in the body.

Draw **one** line from each organ system to its function. [3 marks]
Outcome 2

Organ system	Function
Circulatory system	breaks down food into soluble substances that can enter the blood
Reproductive system	transports oxygen and other substances around the body
Digestive system	produces offspring

c What organ system is the stomach part of?

Tick **one** box. [1 mark]
Outcome 3

☐ circulatory

☐ digestive

☐ nervous

3. Nadia has a cold. She caught it from her friend.

a Use the correct answers from the box to complete each sentence. [2 marks]
Outcome 5

| illness | infectious | microorganisms | people | toxins |

A cold is an _____ disease.

It is caused by _____ called pathogens.

b Nadia feels ill because the pathogens are reproducing in her cells.

This damages the cells.

Which pathogen causes colds?

Tick **one** box. [1 mark]
Outcome 5

☐ antibiotics

☐ bacteria

☐ viruses

4. Steve smokes cigarettes.

a What disease is smoking linked to?

Tick **one** box. [1 mark]
Outcome 4

☐ cancer

☐ liver disease

☐ obesity

b Cigarettes contain a drug called nicotine.

Nicotine is addictive.

What does this mean? [1 mark]
Outcome 7

_____

5. Bacteria cause disease.

What type of cells kill bacteria?

Tick **one** box. [1 mark]
Outcome 6

☐ nerve cells

☐ muscle cells

☐ white blood cells

6. A doctor tests Macey's nervous responses.

He shines a bright light into her eyes.

The diagram shows what happens.

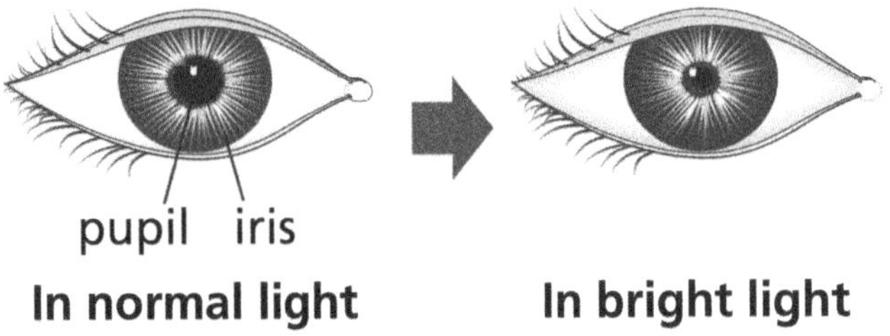

pupil   iris
In normal light   **In bright light**

a What happens to her pupil when the light shines in her eye? [1 mark]
Outcome 8

_____

b This response was fast and automatic. [1 mark]
Outcome 8

What type of response is it? _____

7. The diagram shows a human cell.

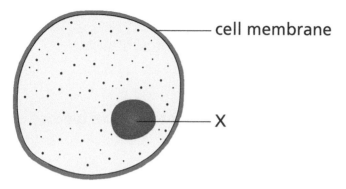

cell membrane

X

a. Name part X. _____ [1 mark]
Outcome 1

b. What is the function of the cell membrane? [1 mark]
Outcome 1

_____

8. The menstrual cycle is controlled by hormones.

a. Use the correct answers from the box to complete each sentence. [2 marks]
Outcome 9

| nerves | glands | chemicals | blood |

Hormones are secreted by _____.

They are transported to their target organs in _____.

b. Hormones are used to increase fertility.

How do they work?

Tick **one** box. [1 mark]
Outcome 10

☐ They inhibit eggs from maturing.

☐ They stimulate eggs to mature.

☐ They inhibit eggs being released.

Total: 20 marks

Outcome 1: Feeding relationships

- The Sun is the source of energy for living organisms.
- Green plants and algae use light to make glucose by photosynthesis.

1. Producers are organisms that use photosynthesis to produce glucose.

Which organisms are producers?

Tick **two** boxes.

☐ oak tree   ☐ fungi   ☐ algae   ☐ bacteria   [2 marks]

2. Photosynthesis is a chemical reaction.

a Use the correct answers from the box to complete the table.   [4 marks]

carbon dioxide   glucose   nitrogen   oxygen   water

Substances that are used in photosynthesis	Substances that are made in photosynthesis

b What else is needed for photosynthesis to take place?

Tick **two** boxes.

☐ soil   ☐ light   ☐ chlorophyll   ☐ food   [2 marks]

3. Connor and Samira changed the distance of a piece of pondweed from a lamp. The diagram shows the equipment they used.

They counted how many oxygen bubbles the pondweed produced in one minute at each distance.

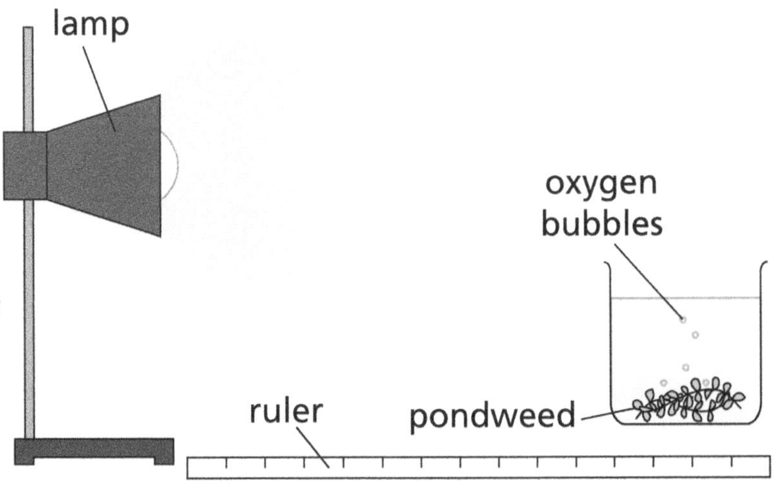

lamp

oxygen bubbles

ruler   pondweed

The table shows their results.

Distance of pondweed from lamp (cm)	Number of oxygen bubbles produced in one minute
10	10
20	7
30	3
40	2
50	1

a Plot the points on the graph axes.

The first one has been done for you. [2 marks]

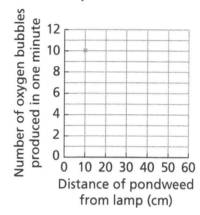

b Draw a line through the points. [1 mark]

c Use the correct answers from the box to complete a conclusion. [2 marks]

decreased   increased   light   oxygen

As the distance of the pondweed from the lamp increased the number of

bubbles of oxygen produced in one minute _____ .

This happened because _____ is needed for
photosynthesis. [2 marks]

4.

GCSE Grade 1

Animals do not carry out photosynthesis but
they still need the Sun to get food. Explain why.

Tip

Plants make their own
food (called glucose) but
animals need to eat to
get their food.

_____

_____ [2 marks]

Outcome 2: Adaptation

- Some animals and plants have special features that help them survive in the conditions where they normally live.
- This means they are adapted to their environment.

1. Cacti are plants that live in the desert.

a Use the correct answers from the box.

adapted	habit	habitat	survival

The desert is a _____ for cacti.

Cacti have special features so they can survive there. This means

that they are _____ . [2 marks]

b This is a cactus.

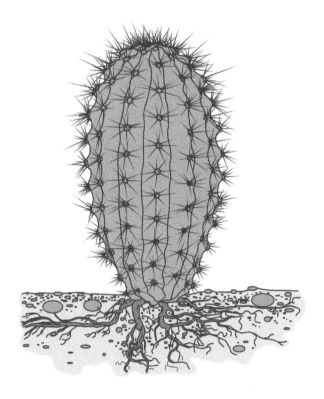

Describe one adaptation it has.

_____ [1 mark]

2. Polar bears are adapted to live in the Arctic.

The column on the left lists polar bear adaptations.

The column on the right lists the function of the adaptations.

Draw **one** line from each adaptation to its function.

Adaptation

| White fur |

| Thick fur |

| Sharp claws |

Function of adaptation

| to kill prey |

| to keep warm |

| for camouflage |

[3 marks]

3. Carly wanted to answer the question 'Why do polar bears have fur?'

GCSE Grade 1

She used two glass beakers. She wrapped one with fur.

She added warm water to each beaker.

She measured the temperature of the water in each beaker and then again after five minutes.

The table shows her results.

Beaker	Temperature at start (°C)	Temperature after five minutes (°C)	Temperature change (°C)
With fur	52	35	17
With no fur	52	26	

a What is the temperature change for the beaker with no fur?

_____°C   [1 mark]

b Use the results to answer Carly's question.

_____

_____

_____ [2 marks]

33

Outcome 3: Food chains and webs

- Feeding relationships in an ecosystem can be shown using a food chain.
- All food chains begin with a producer.
- A food web shows how food chains in an ecosystem are linked.

1. This is a food chain.

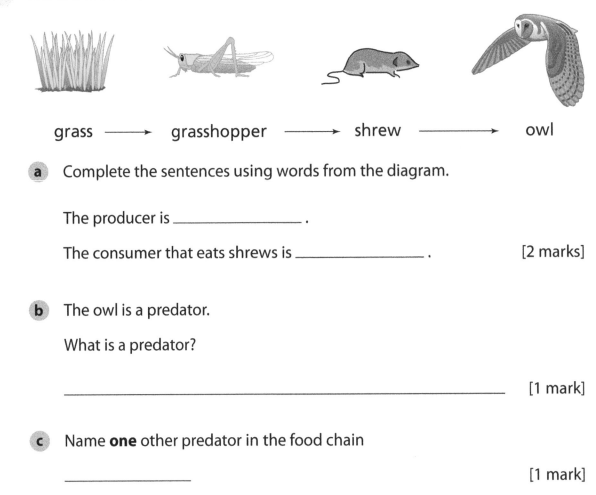

grass ⟶ grasshopper ⟶ shrew ⟶ owl

a Complete the sentences using words from the diagram.

The producer is _____ .

The consumer that eats shrews is _____ . [2 marks]

b The owl is a predator.

What is a predator?

_____ [1 mark]

c Name **one** other predator in the food chain

_____ [1 mark]

2. Food chains in an ecosystem are connected into a food web.

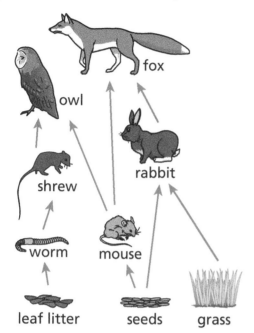

Tip

An ecosystem is all the plants and animals that live in an area as well as the place where they live.

a Mice are prey for which organisms?

Tick **two** boxes.

☐ rabbits   ☐ foxes

☐ owls   ☐ seeds   [2 marks]

b Foxes are top predators in this ecosystem.

What does this mean?

_____ [1 mark]

c The number of worms increases.

What happens to the number of shrews?

_____ [1 mark]

3.

GCSE Grade 1

The amount of seeds in the food chain from question 2 decreases.

Why does this affect the mice more than rabbits?

Tip

Use the food web to work out what mice and rabbits eat.

_____ [1 mark]

Outcome 4: Recycling materials

- All materials in the natural world are recycled.
- This provides materials to build new organisms.
- Decay of dead plants and animals by microorganisms returns carbon to the atmosphere as carbon dioxide.

1. Living things use materials from the environment for growth and other processes.

   Use the correct answers from the box to complete each sentence.

animals	die	eat	microorganisms

   Materials are returned to the environment in waste materials or when living

   things _____ and decay.

   Materials decay because they are broken down (digested)

   by _____ .   [2 marks]

2. Autumn leaves decay.

   What conditions cause them to decay the fastest?

   Tick **one** box.

   ☐ warm and dry   ☐ warm and damp

   ☐ cold and dry   ☐ cold and damp   [1 mark]

3. The diagram shows how carbon is recycled. This is called the carbon cycle.

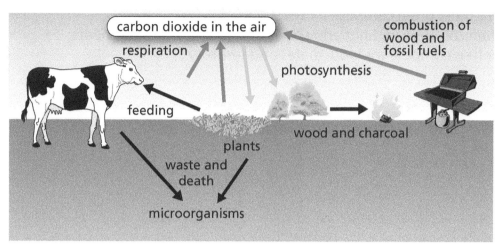

a Which process removes carbon dioxide from the air?

Tick **one** box.

Tip

The arrows show the movement of carbon.

☐ respiration ☐ feeding

☐ combustion ☐ photosynthesis [1 mark]

b Name one process that returns carbon to the air.

_____ [1 mark]

c How does carbon move from plants to animals?

_____ [1 mark]

4. When grapes decay, they break down to form liquid.

GCSE Grade 1

Davin wants to find out if grapes decay faster at a warm temperature.

Describe a method that he could use.

_____

_____

_____ [2 marks]

Outcome 5: Competition

- Organisms must often compete for resources.
- Plants often compete for light and space, and for water and nutrients.
- Animals often compete for food, mates and territory.

1. Which of these resources do animals compete for?

   Tick **two** boxes.

   ☐ food   ☐ mates

   ☐ light   ☐ soil nutrients   [2 marks]

2. Cheetahs and lions are big cats that live in the same habitat.

   a Which sentence describes competition between the cheetahs and lions?

   Tip
   A habitat is a place where something lives.

   Tick **one** box.

   ☐ Lions and cheetahs mate to produce offspring.

   ☐ Both lions and cheetahs eat antelopes.

   ☐ Both lions and cheetahs breathe air.

   ☐ Antelopes eat grass.   [1 mark]

   b 'Cheetahs compete with other cheetahs.'

   Is this sentence true or false?

   _____   [1 mark]

3. Saffia planted 10 plants in a flower pot. The plants all died.

   Use the correct answers from the box to complete the paragraph to explain why.   [2 marks]

compete	food	grow	water

   The plants had to _____ for resources.

   There were not enough nutrients and _____ for all of the plants.

4. Fin noticed a plant called ivy growing up a tree.

Which resource does this help the ivy to get?

Tick **one** box.

☐ water   ☐ nutrients

☐ mates   ☐ light   [1 mark]

---

5. Some forests in the UK are home to both red and grey squirrels. They are different species.

GCSE Grade 1

Both types of squirrel eat acorns.

Grey squirrels are larger than red squirrels.

> **Tip**
>
> Red and grey squirrels are different species so they cannot breed with each other.

a Name one resource that red and grey squirrels compete for.

_____ [1 mark]

b Use the information in the question to explain why there are many more grey squirrels than red squirrels in the UK.

_____

_____ [2 marks]

Outcome 6: Abiotic and biotic factors

- Animals and plants are affected by both biotic and abiotic factors.
- Non-living factors are abiotic.
- Living factors are biotic.
- A species is extinct if no individuals of the species remain.

1. Living organisms are affected by different factors.

The column on the left lists some keywords.

The column on the right lists their meanings.

Draw **one** line from each word to its meaning.

Keyword	**Meaning**
Environment	the surroundings that an organism lives in
Abiotic factor	a living factor of an ecosystem
Biotic factor	a non-living factor of an ecosystem

[3 marks]

2. Factors that affect animals and plants can be biotic or abiotic.

Which are abiotic factors?

Tick **two** boxes.

☐ temperature ☐ number of predators

☐ soil type ☐ a disease caused by bacteria [2 marks]

3. This graph shows how an abiotic factor on Earth has changed.

a Use the correct answers from the box to complete each sentence.

> **weather decreased increased temperature**

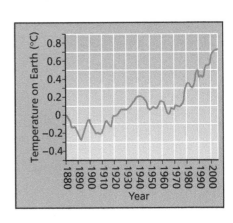

40

The graph shows that the _____ on Earth has changed.

It has _____ over time. [2 marks]

b This change is causing ice in the North Pole to melt. This makes it difficult for polar bears to survive.

Complete this sentence.

In the future there may be no polar bears. This means they will be _____ . [1 mark]

4. Noah wants to find out if the abiotic factors in his garden are the same everywhere.

The drawing shows the view of his garden from above.

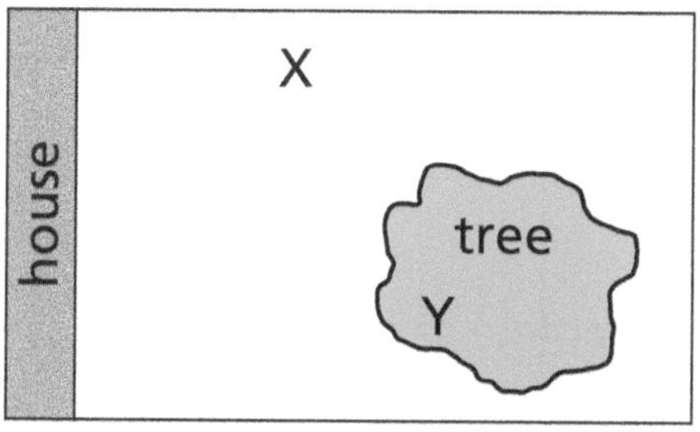

Noah measures the light intensity at point X.

Predict how the light intensity will be different at point Y.

Give a reason why you think this.

Tip
Light intensity means amount of light.

_____

_____ [2 marks]

5. Foxes and rabbits live in a field.

GCSE Grade 1

Foxes are predators of rabbits.

The foxes all get a disease, which kills them.

What will happen to the number of rabbits?

Give a reason for your answer.

_____

_____ [2 marks]

Outcome 7: Pollution

- Human population is increasing. This causes more resources to be used and more waste to be produced.
- Human activity causes pollution.
- Pollution can affect the water, air and land.

1. Pollution can affect the water, air and land.

   Which causes air pollution?

   Tick **two** boxes.

   Tip
   Air pollution is caused by gases or small particles.

   ☐ sulfur dioxide   ☐ sewage

   ☐ fertilisers   ☐ smoke   [2 marks]

2. Acid rain kills living organisms.

   Use the correct answers from the box to complete each sentence.

air	oxygen	smoke	sulfur

   [2 marks]

   When fuels are burnt _____ and gases are released.

   A gas called _____ dioxide dissolves in rainwater to make acid rain.

3. Humans cause pollution in different ways.

   The column on the left lists some keywords.

   The column on the right lists meanings.

   Draw **one** line from each keyword to its meaning.

Keyword	Meaning
Sewage	a toxic substance used to kill pests
Herbicide	waste material that contains faeces and urine
Pesticide	a toxic chemical used to kill weeds

   [3 marks]

4. **a** Use the correct answer from the box to complete this sentence.

| deforestation | landfill | pollution |

Humans cut down trees and remove them. This is called

_____ . [1 mark]

b Why do humans do this?

Give **one** reason.

_____ [1 mark]

5. Alex and Zaynab investigated how pollution changes as you move away from a road.

GCSE Grade 1

They used a piece of damp cotton wool to wipe some leaves found high up on trees close to a busy road.

The cotton wool was very dirty.

They then repeated this for leaves found far away from the road.

a What do you think they will see on the leaves found far away from the road?

_____ [1 mark]

b Explain why you think this.

_____ [1 mark]

Outcome 8: Evolution

- Charles Darwin's theory of evolution says that living things evolved from simple life forms that lived three billion years ago.
- Natural selection explains how evolution happens.
- Artificial selection is also called selective breeding. Humans choose which plants and animals to breed together for useful characteristics.

1. Species living today descended from those living in the past. This is evolution.

Use the correct answers from the box to complete each sentence.

artificial	complex	Darwin	natural	simple

Evolution can be explained by a theory called _____ selection.

This theory was suggested by a scientist called Charles _____ .

He said that all living things have evolved from _____
life forms. [3 marks]

2. The horses alive today evolved from other horse species.

The diagrams show this, and the changes to the bones in the horses' feet.

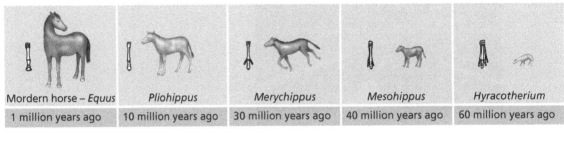

Mordern horse – Equus	Pliohippus	Merychippus	Mesohippus	Hyracotherium
1 million years ago	10 million years ago	30 million years ago	40 million years ago	60 million years ago

a What did scientists use to work this out?

Tick **one** box.

☐ microscopes   ☐ photographs

☐ fossils   ☐ theories   [1 mark]

b How have the species changed as the horse evolved?

Tick **two** boxes.

☐ increased height   ☐ decreased height

☐ increased number of toes   ☐ decreased number
of toes   [2 marks]

3. Joe owns many racing greyhounds.

Some are faster than others.

a Complete this sentence.

Joe chooses which dogs to breed together. This is an example

of _____ selection. [1 mark]

b He wants the puppies that are born to run fast.

What should he do to achieve this?

_____ [1 mark]

4. Peppered moths spend most of the day resting on tree bark.

pale variety

dark variety

There are two varieties of peppered moth.

One is pale and the other is dark. Both varieties live in a forest where the tree bark is pale.

a Why are there more pale moths than dark?

_____

_____ [2 marks]

b The forest becomes polluted. The tree bark gets darker.

Predict what will happen to the numbers of each colour moth.

Tip
You need to say what you think will happen.

_____

_____ [2 marks]

c Complete the sentence.

Changes to the populations of the two varieties of peppered moth are

an example of _____ selection. [1 mark]

Outcome 9: Reproduction

- Reproduction produces offspring. There are two types of reproduction.
- In sexual reproduction male and female sex cells join.
- In asexual reproduction there is only one parent.

1.   Most animals use sexual reproduction.

Which are animal sex cells?

Tick **two** boxes.

☐ egg   ☐ offspring

☐ pollen   ☐ sperm   [2 marks]

2.   During sexual reproduction sex cells join.

Use the correct answers from the box to complete each sentence.

genetic   offspring   parents   reproduction

When sex cells join there is a mixing of _____ information.

This leads to variety in the _____ .   [2 marks]

3.   A strawberry plant produces
a stem called a runner.

A new plant develops at the
end of the runner. This is an
example of asexual reproduction.

new plant
(offspring)

Which sentence is true?

Tick **one** box.

parent plant   runner

☐ The new plant has the
same characteristics as
the parent plant.

☐ The new plant has half of the same characteristics as the parent plant.

☐ The new plant has different characteristics to the parent plant.   [1 mark]

4. Ali took a cutting from a plant.

He cut off a stem from a plant. Then planted this into a pot of soil.

The cutting grew into a new plant, which was a clone.

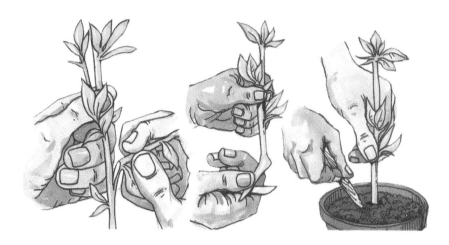

A clone has the same characteristics as the parent.

a Complete this sentence:

Taking cuttings is a type of _____ reproduction.   [1 mark]

b Is this method of creating new plants quicker or slower than

planting seeds? _____   [1 mark]

5. The gene for fur colour in mice has two different versions – grey and white.

GCSE Grade 1

Grey fur is shown by the letter **F**. White fur is shown by the letter **f**.

A male and female mouse both have the genes **Ff**. They have grey fur.

The mice breed and have babies.

Some of the babies are white. Explain why.

Tip

The mice breed using sexual reproduction. The offspring receive one gene from each parent.

_____

_____   [2 marks]

Outcome 10: DNA, genes and chromosomes

- Genetic material is made of DNA. This is contained in structures called chromosomes.
- Chromosomes carry genes that control the characteristics of the body.
- Humans have 23 pairs of chromosomes.
- In genetic engineering, genes from one organism are 'cut out' and transferred to the cells of another organism.

1. Use the correct answers from the box to label the diagram.   [4 marks]

| cell membrane   chromosome   DNA   gene   nucleus |

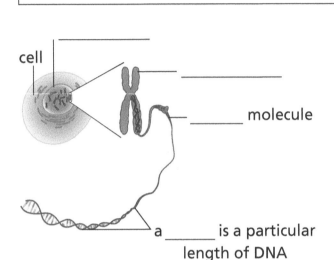

cell

_____ molecule

a _____ is a particular
length of DNA

2. How many chromosomes do humans have?

Tip
Humans have 23 pairs of chromosomes.

Tick **one** box.

☐ 23   ☐ 32   ☐ 46   ☐ 64   [1 mark]

3. One pair of chromosomes carries the genes that determine sex.

Use the correct answers from the box to complete each sentence.

| same   short   XY   YZ |

Females have the _____ sex chromosomes. They are XX.

In males the chromosomes are different. They are _____ .   [2 marks]

4. Genetic engineering is used to make bacteria that can make a human hormone called insulin.

Write numbers 1–4 in the boxes to show the order in which this is done.

We have done the first one to help you.

The insulin gene is cut out.	☐
Scientists find the gene for insulin in human DNA.	1
The bacteria reproduces many times and produces insulin.	☐
The insulin gene is inserted into the bacteria's DNA.	☐

[3 marks]

5. Genetic engineering can also be used to change the genes in plants that we eat (crops).

Some people are against this.

Give one reason why.

_____ [1 mark]

6. The 24 students in a class measured their height and arm span.

GCSE Grade 1

They put their results on a scatter graph. Each circle shows one student.

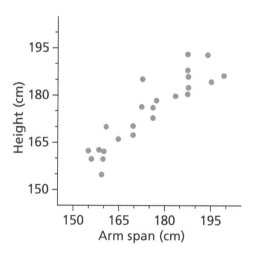

height

arm span

Tip

You need to describe the relationship between height and arm span. Start your answer: 'Taller people have …'.

Describe the pattern. [1 mark]

_____

Mini test

1. Alligators eat turtles. Turtles eat algae.

a Write the organisms into the correct boxes below, to form a simple food chain.

[1 mark]
Outcome 3

b Name the producer in the food chain. _____

[1 mark]
Outcome 3

2. Green plants and algae use photosynthesis to make glucose.

Use the correct answers from the box to complete the word equation for photosynthesis.

[2 marks]
Outcome 2

energy	light	oxygen	water

Carbon dioxide + _____ → _____ + glucose

3. A group of nettle plants are growing under a tree.

a What are the plants competing for?

Tick **one** box.

[1 mark]
Outcome 5

☐ light ☐ mates ☐ heat

b Which is a living factor that affects the growth of the plants?

Tick **one** box.

[1 mark]
Outcome 6

☐ insects that eat plants

☐ temperature

☐ amount of rain

4. Reproduction is sexual or asexual.

a Which sentence describes sexual reproduction?

Tick **one** box.

[1 mark]
Outcome 9

☐ There is a mixing of genetic information, which leads to variety in the offspring.

☐ There is no mixing of genetic information, which leads to identical offspring.

☐ There is a mixing of genetic information, which leads to identical offspring.

b Which type of reproduction involves the joining of sex cells?

_____

[1 mark]
Outcome 9

c Name the male sex cells in animals.

_____

[1 mark]
Outcome 9

5. Cheetahs are predators. In a group of cheetahs, some are fast and some are slow.

a The fast cheetahs will survive. The slow cheetahs will die.

Why?

Tick **one** box. [1 mark]
Outcome 5

☐ The fast cheetahs will be able to run away from predators.

☐ The slow cheetahs will not get enough food.

☐ The fast cheetahs will catch more mates.

b Use the correct answers from the box to complete the sentence. [2 marks]
Outcome 10

| cells genes offspring parents reproduction |

The fast cheetahs survive and breed.

They pass on _____ for fast speed to their _____ .

c This is an example of natural selection. [1 mark]
Outcome 8

Which scientist used natural selection to explain how living organisms evolve?

_____

6. Living organisms may be adapted for survival in their environment.

The column on the left lists living organisms.

The column on the right lists adaptations.

Draw **one** line from each living organism to its adaptation. [3 marks]
Outcome 2

Living organism

| Cactus |

| Polar bear |

| Shark |

Adaptation

| thick layer of fat for warmth |

| can store water |

| gills for breathing |

7. In 1911, there were 45 million people living in the UK.

By 2011, this had increased by 18 million people.

a How many people lived in the UK in 2011?

_____ million

[1 mark]
Outcome 7

b This increase in the number of people results in more waste being made.

Some waste is put into landfill sites.

What do landfill sites produce?

Tick **one** box.

[1 mark]
Outcome 7

☐ Toxic chemicals that pollute the land.

☐ Sulfur dioxide that pollutes the air.

☐ Herbicides that pollute the water.

8. All materials in the living world are recycled to provide the

building blocks for future organisms.

[2 marks]
Outcome 4

Use the correct answers from the box to complete each sentence.

animals feeding microorganisms photosynthesis respiration

The decay of dead plants and animals by _____ returns carbon to the atmosphere as carbon dioxide.

This is removed from the atmosphere when used by plants in _____ .

Total: 20 marks

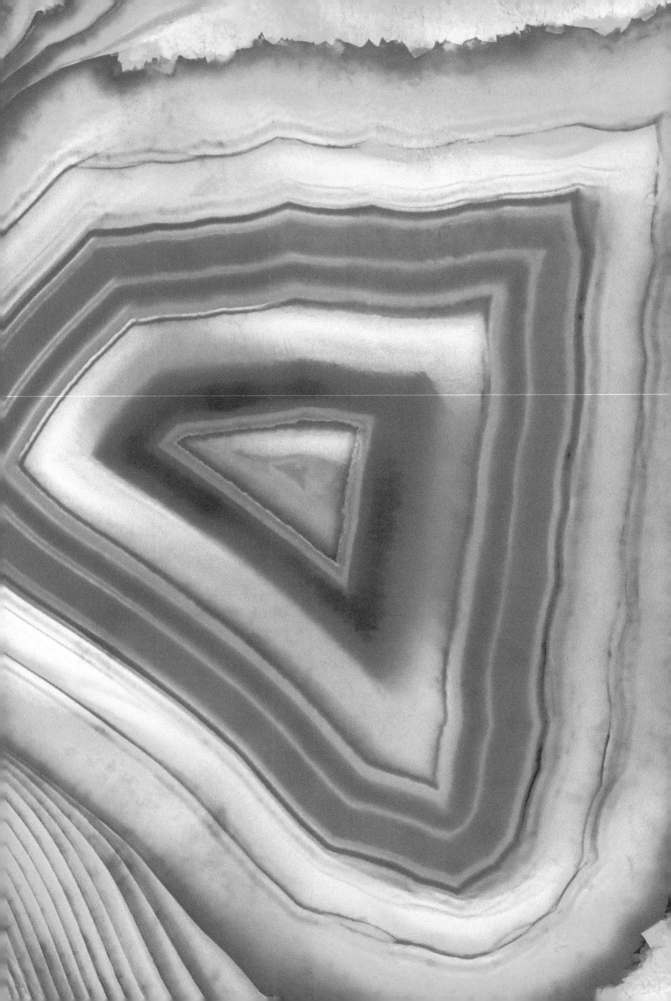

CHEMISTRY

Outcome 1: Atoms and elements

- All substances are made from atoms.
- An element is made from only one sort of atom.
- The Periodic table shows all the known elements.
- Elements in the same group of the Periodic table have similar chemical properties.
- Most elements are metals.
- The properties of metals are usually different from the properties of non-metals.

1.   What is an atom?

Tick **one** box.

☐ A metal in the Periodic table.

☐ The smallest part of an element that can exist.

☐ The smallest non-metal that can be found.   [1 mark]

2.   The diagram shows **part** of the Periodic table.

Groups

1	2										3	4	5	6	7	0
						H										He
Li	Be										B	C	N	O	F	Ne
Na	Mg										Al	Si	P	S	Cl	Ar
K	Ca	Sc	Ti	V	Cr	Mn	Fe	Co	Ni	Cu	Zn	Ga	Ge	As	Se	Br	Kr
Rb	Sr	Y	Zr	Nb	Mo	Tc	Ru	Rh	Pd	Ag	Cd	In	Sn	Sb	Te	I	Xe

Use the correct answers from the box to complete each sentence.

75	100	200	Cl	He	Rb

There are about _____ elements in the complete Periodic table.

The chemical symbol for one of the metals in the Periodic table is

_____.

The chemical symbol for one of the elements in Group 7

is _____.   [3 marks]

3. Iron and copper are metals. Sulfur and oxygen are non-metals.

Complete the table to show the physical properties of metals and non-metals.

Put **one** tick in each correct box.

We have done one to help you.

	Metals	Non-metals
Shiny		
Low boiling point		
Weak when solid		✔
Good conductor of heat		
Poor conductor of electricity		

[4 marks]

4. Antimony is an element used in the manufacture of plastic for drinks bottles.

Antimony has these properties:

- it does not conduct heat easily
- it has a high melting point
- it has a low strength
- it is shiny.

Give **two** reasons why we cannot be sure that antimony is a metal.

_____

_____ [2 marks]

Outcome 2: Making compounds

- Atoms join with other atoms when elements react.
- A compound is formed when two or more different elements react together.
- Compounds like sodium chloride are made from a metal and a non-metal.
- Compounds like carbon dioxide are made from non-metals only.
- Word equations show what happens in chemical reactions.

1. Which of these sentences is correct?

Tick **one** box.

☐ Atoms are made of elements.

☐ Elements are made of compounds.

☐ Compounds are made of elements. [1 mark]

2. The diagram shows the atoms in three different substances.

Each different atom has a different colour.

A   B   C   D

Which **two** of these substances are compounds?

Tick **one** box.

☐ B and D

☐ A and C

☐ A and D [1 mark]

3. Use the correct answer from the box to complete the sentence.

an atom	a mixture	a compound	an element

Copper oxide is _____. [1 mark]

4. The column on the left lists some compounds.

The column on the right lists some descriptions of compounds.

Draw **one** line from each compound to its description.

We have done one to help you.

Compound	Description
Carbon dioxide	
Sodium chloride	metal and non-metal combined
Silicon dioxide ————	**non-metals combined**
Iron oxide	

[3 marks]

5. Magnesium reacts with oxygen to produce magnesium oxide.

Complete the table to show if a substance is a reactant or a product in the reaction.

Put **one** tick in each correct box.

	Reactant	Product
Oxygen		
Magnesium		
Magnesium oxide		

[3 marks]

6. Complete the word equation for the reaction between two non-metals to produce sulfur dioxide.

_____ + _____ → sulfur dioxide   [1 mark]

7. Write word equations for these reactions.

a Iron reacting with chlorine to produce iron chloride.

_____   [1 mark]

b Carbon reacting with oxygen to produce carbon dioxide.

_____   [1 mark]

Outcome 3: States of matter

- The states of matter are solid, liquid and gas.
- Substances melt or freeze at their melting point.
- Substances boil or condense at their boiling point.
- The particles in a substance can be shown as solid spheres.
- Kinetic theory is an idea that describes how these particles are arranged and move.
- The arrangement and movement of particles change during state changes.

1. The column on the left lists the states of matter.

   The column on the right shows diagrams of particle arrangements.

   Draw **one** line from each state of matter to the correct diagram. [3 marks]

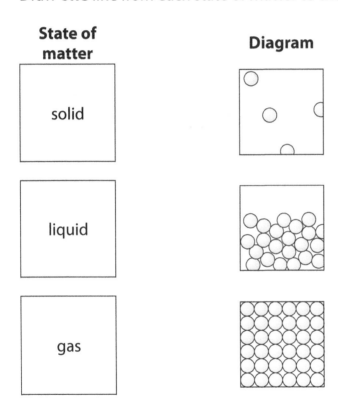

2. Use the correct answers from the box to complete the sentences.

boils	condenses	freezes	melts

   A substance _____ when it changes from a solid to a liquid.

   A substance _____ when it changes from a gas to a liquid. [2 marks]

3. Ethanol is a liquid at room temperature. It is used in some antiseptic hand gels.

What happens to ethanol at its boiling point?

Tick **one** box.

☐ It can only boil.

☐ It can condense or boil.

☐ It can only condense.

[1 mark]

4. Complete the table to show the arrangement and movement of particles in each state of matter.

Put **one** tick in each correct box.

We have done one to help you.

[4 marks]

	Solid	Liquid	Gas
Particles are close together			
Particles are in fixed positions			
Particles can change places		✔	
Particles can move about at high speed			

5. What happens to the particles in a liquid when the liquid boils?

Tick **one** box.

☐ They move far apart and begin to move around rapidly.

☐ They stay close together and begin to move around rapidly.

☐ They move close together and become able to move around. [1 mark]

6. Write down what happens to the arrangement and movement of particles when a solid melts.

GCSE Grade 1

Arrangement:

_____

Movement:

_____ [2 marks]

Outcome 4: Diamond and graphite

- Carbon is a non-metal element.
- Diamond and graphite are two different forms of carbon.
- Diamond and graphite have different structures and properties.
- The structures of diamond and graphite explain their properties.

1. Complete the table to show the properties of diamond and graphite.

   Put **one** tick in each correct box.

	Diamond	Graphite
Soft		
Hard		
Slippery		

   [3 marks]

2. The diagrams show two different forms of carbon.

   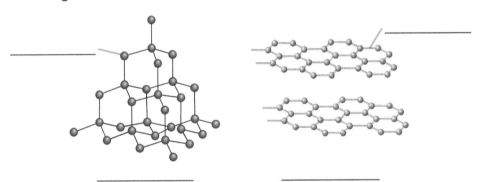

   Use the correct answers from the box to label the diagrams.   [4 marks]

carbon atom   diamond   graphite   strong bond   weak bond

3. Use the correct answers from the box to complete the sentences.

bonds   carbon   chlorine   giant   layers   small

   Diamond and graphite are made from _____ atoms.

   The atoms in diamond are joined in a _____ three-dimensional structure.

   The atoms in graphite are joined together in _____ .   [3 marks]

4. Concrete is a very strong material.

The photo shows holes being drilled in a concrete wall.

The drill bit has tiny diamonds attached to its cutting edge.

a Why is diamond used for some drill bits?

Tick **one** box.

☐ It is transparent.

☐ It is expensive.

☐ It is very hard. [1 mark]

b Write down one other use of diamond.

_____ [1 mark]

5. Graphite is used in pencils.

Why is graphite soft?

Tick **one** box.

☐ It has layers that can slide over each other.

☐ Its atoms can slide around each other.

☐ It has three-dimensional atoms. [1 mark]

6. Diamond and graphite have different structures.

GCSE Grade 1

Describe how to tell diagrams of the structure of diamond and graphite apart.

_____

_____ [2 marks]

Outcome 5: Separating mixtures

- A mixture contains two or more different substances.
- The different substances in a mixture are not chemically joined together.
- Different methods are used to separate different kinds of mixtures.
- Separation methods include crystallisation, chromatography, distillation and filtration.

1. The diagrams show the atoms in different materials.

   Which diagram shows a mixture?

   A   B   C

   Tick **one** box.

   ☐ A   ☐ B   ☐ C   [1 mark]

2. Which statement about mixtures is correct?

   Tick **one** box.

   ☐ All mixtures are liquids.

   ☐ Mixtures are always solids or liquids.

   ☐ Mixtures can be solids, liquids or gases.   [1 mark]

3. Complete the table to show if a substance is a pure substance or a mixture.

   Put **one** tick in each correct box.

	Pure substance	Mixture
Air		
Gold		
Seawater		

   [3 marks]

4. The column on the left shows two diagrams.

The column on the right lists four separation methods.

Draw **one** line from each diagram to the correct separation method.   [2 marks]

Diagram	**Separation method**

Crystallisation

Chromatography

Distillation

Filtration

5. Use the correct answers from the box to complete the sentences.   [4 marks]

chromatography   **crystallisation**   **distillation**   **filtration**   **stirring**

Sugar can be separated from sugar solution using _____.

_____ is used to get pure water from salty water.

Sand can be separated from a mixture of sand and water using _____.

_____ is used to separate different coloured inks.

6. A teacher has a mixture of broken glass and copper sulfate in a beaker.

The teacher adds water to dissolve the copper sulfate.

Write down **two** separation methods, in the order needed, to produce

pure dry copper sulfate. _____ then _____   [2 marks]

Outcome 6: Paper chromatography

- Paper chromatography is used to separate mixtures of soluble compounds.
- Paper chromatography can be used to identify a compound in a mixture.
- A liquid solvent moves through the paper, carrying compounds with it.
- Different compounds travel different distances through the paper.
- A compound can be identified by its colour and the distance it travels.

1. Which of these mixtures can be separated using paper chromatography?

Tick **one** box.

☐ A mixture of table salt and sugar.

☐ A mixture of food dyes for a cake.

☐ A mixture of orange juice and lemon juice. [1 mark]

2. The diagram shows a simple paper chromatography experiment.

Use the correct answers from the box to label the diagram. [4 marks]

| paper   sample spot   solvent   test tube |

_____

_____

_____

pencil line

_____

3. The sentences with the boxes describe a chromatography experiment.

The order of the steps is incorrect.

Write a number (1–5) in each box to show the correct order.

We have done the first step for you.

Draw a pencil line near the bottom of the paper. ☐ 1

Put the paper in the solvent. ☐

Take the paper out before the solvent reaches the top. ☐

Put a small spot of the mixture on the pencil line. ☐

Let the solvent move through the paper. ☐ [3 marks]

4. A student used paper chromatography to separate four different inks (A, B, C and D).

The diagram shows the student's results.

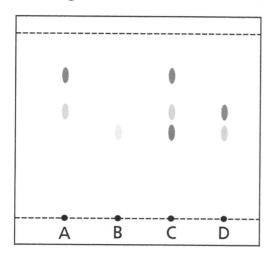

Use the correct letters (A, B, C, D) to answer the questions.

a Which ink contained only one compound? _____

b Which ink contained three different compounds? _____

c Which **two** inks contained two identical compounds? _____

and _____   [4 marks]

5. A solvent is a substance that can dissolve other substances.

GCSE Grade 1

a The line at the bottom of the paper in question 4 is drawn using a pencil.

Give a reason why the line is not drawn using a pen.

_____ [1 mark]

b The sample spot must not be below the solvent level at the start.

Give a reason why the sample spot must be above the solvent level.

_____ [1 mark]

Outcome 7: Extracting metals

- Ores contain profitable amounts of metal.
- Ores are obtained by mining and quarrying.
- Metals are extracted from ores in different ways.
- More reactive metals are more difficult to extract from their ores.
- Recycling metals saves resources and reduces damage to the environment.

1. Use the correct answer from the box to complete the sentence.

difficult	**economic**	**expensive**	**reactive**

An ore contains enough metal to make it _____ to extract
a metal. [1 mark]

2. The diagram shows five metals in order of reactivity.

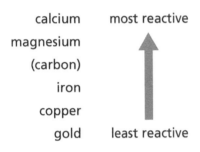

calcium   most reactive
magnesium
(carbon)
iron
copper
gold   least reactive

Carbon is shown in brackets because it is a non-metal.

Choose metals from the diagram when you answer
questions **a** and **b** below.

a Give the name of **one** metal that is less reactive than carbon.

_____ [1 mark]

b Give the name of **one** metal that is more reactive than carbon.

_____ [1 mark]

c Which of these metals is extracted from its ore by heating with carbon?

Tick **one** box.

☐ iron   ☐ calcium   ☐ gold   [1 mark]

3. Why is gold found in the Earth as the metal itself, rather than as a compound?

Tick **one** box.

☐ It is unreactive.

☐ It is shiny.

☐ It is very valuable.

[1 mark]

4. The sentences describe how zinc ore in the Earth is turned into zinc metal.

The order of the steps is incorrect.

Write a number (1–4) in each box to show the correct order.

Purify the zinc. ☐

Heat the zinc ore with carbon. ☐

Mine large amounts of rocks that contain zinc ore. ☐

Separate the zinc ore from the rocks. ☐

[3 marks]

5. Which of these is a reason why we should recycle metals?

Tick **one** box.

☐ To increase waste and energy use.

☐ To take jobs away from miners.

☐ To reduce the need to quarry ores.

[1 mark]

6. Give **two** ways in which getting ores from the Earth harms the environment.

GCSE Grade 1

_____

_____ [2 marks]

Outcome 8: Metals

- The atoms in metals are arranged in giant structures.
- There are strong bonds between metal atoms.
- Metals have high melting points because of the strong bonds.
- Metals are good conductors of thermal energy and electricity.
- Aluminium and copper have different uses because they have different properties.

1. Each circle in the diagram shows a metal atom.

The atoms are part of the structure of solid copper.

Complete the diagram by drawing four more copper atoms.

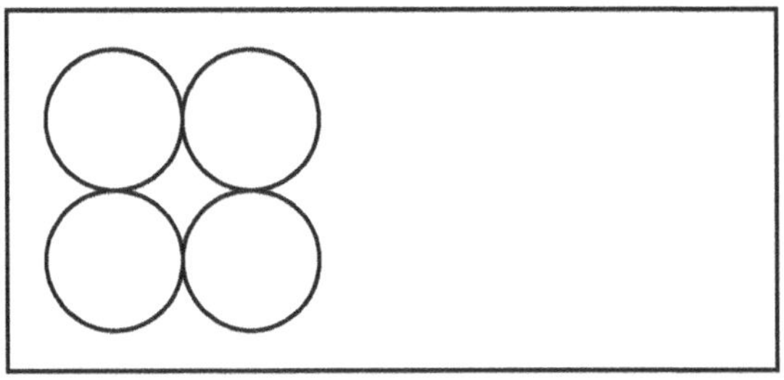

[2 marks]

2. Why do metals have high melting points?

Tick **one** box.

☐ They are made of atoms.

☐ There are strong bonds between the atoms.

☐ They are good conductors of thermal energy. [1 mark]

3. The table shows the densities of three different metals.

Metal	Density (g/cm³)
Aluminium	2.7
Copper	9.0
Sodium	0.9

Which metal has the lowest density?

Tick **one** box.

☐ aluminium   ☐ copper   ☐ sodium   [1 mark]

4. Use the correct answer from the box to complete the sentence.

conduction	corrosion	extraction	insulation

The process that happens when air and water break down a metal is called

_____ . [1 mark]

5. Metals have properties that make them suitable for different uses.

The column on the left lists some properties.

The column on the right lists some uses.

Draw **one** line from each property to the correct use.

We have done one to help you. [2 marks]

Property **Use**

jewellery

Conducts electricity easily and is easily bent

aircraft parts

Unreactive and shiny

electrical wiring

Low density and resists corrosion

bridges

6. Plumbing is the system of pipes that carries hot and cold water in homes.

Which of these metals is the most suitable for plumbing?

Tick **one** box.

☐ copper ☐ iron ☐ sodium [1 mark]

7. Very long outdoor electricity cables are made from aluminium.

GCSE Grade 1

Give **two** properties of aluminium that make it suitable
for making these cables.

1. _____

_____

2. _____

_____ [2 marks]

Outcome 9: Alloys

- Pure aluminium, iron, and gold are too soft for many uses.
- An alloy is a mixture of a metal with other elements and not a compound.
- Alloys of aluminium, iron and gold are harder than the pure metals.
- Steels are alloys of iron and carbon with other metals.
- Most metals are converted into alloys for everyday use.

1. Car engines are made from metal.

The pie chart shows the substances found in this metal.

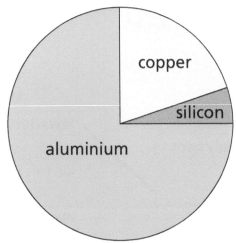

a Why are other elements mixed with aluminium to make this metal?

Tick **one** box.

☐ To make the metal shinier.

☐ To make the metal harder.

☐ To make the metal melt easily. [1 mark]

b What type of substance is this metal?

Draw a circle around the correct answer. [1 mark]

alloy   compound   pure metal   solution

c What is the percentage of silicon in this metal?

Tick **one** box.

☐ 5%   ☐ 20%   ☐ 25% [1 mark]

2. Gold alloys are used to make jewellery.

The hardness of gold alloys changes with the percentage of other metals in them.

The graph shows how the hardness of gold alloys changes.

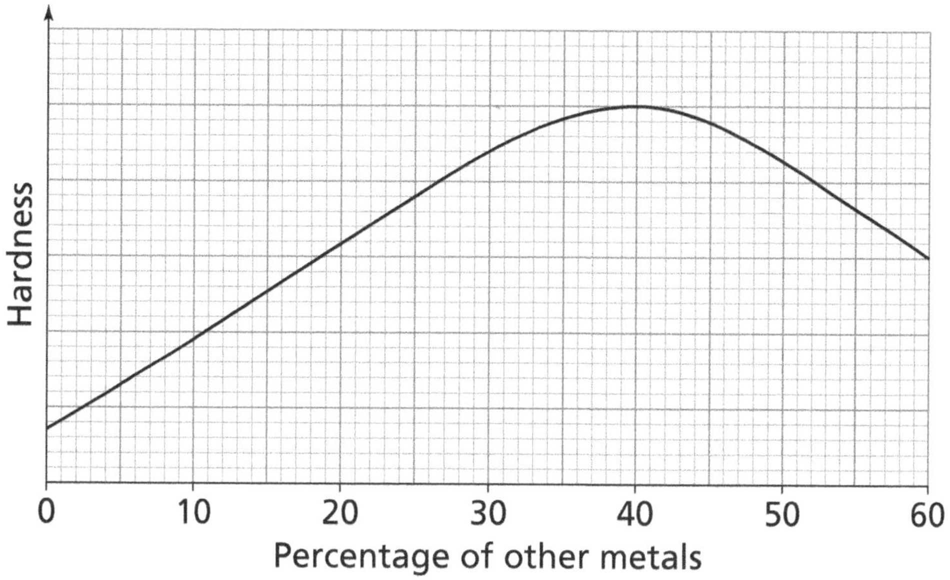

What percentage of other metals makes the hardest gold alloy?

_____ %   [1 mark]

3. Steels are used to make cars, bridges, buildings and ships.

What are steels?

Tick **one** box.

Compounds of iron, carbon and other metals. ☐

Iron mixed with carbon and other metals. ☐

Different types of pure iron. ☐   [1 mark]

4. Give a reason that explains why most iron is converted into steels.

GCSE Grade 1

_____

_____ [2 marks]

Outcome 10: Polymers

- Monomers are small compounds that join together to form very long chains.
- The substances with very long chains are called polymers.
- PVC, poly(ethene), poly(propene) and polystyrene are polymers.
- Polymers have many everyday uses because they have useful properties.
- Polymers do not break down easily. This leads to problems with waste.

1. The diagram shows how poly(ethene) is made.

Lots of ethene molecules

Molecule of poly(ethene)

a Which of the following sentences is correct?

Tick **one** box.

☐ Ethene and poly(ethene) are both polymers.

☐ Ethene is a monomer and poly(ethene) is a polymer.

☐ Ethene is a polymer and poly(ethene) is a monomer.　　[1 mark]

b Which of these is a property of poly(ethene)?

Tick **one** box.

☐ Breaks when folded.

☐ Dissolves in water.

☐ Not affected by acids and alkalis.　　[1 mark]

2. Poly(ethene) is used to make polythene food wrappings, containers and pipes.

Use the correct answers from the box to complete the sentences.

cooled	dissolved	heated	moulded	rolled

a Poly(ethene) softens when _____ .

b Poly(ethene) can be _____ into sheets to make shopping bags.

c Poly(ethene) can be _____ to make buckets.　　[3 marks]

3. Many polymers are difficult to dispose of because they are not biodegradable.

What is a biodegradable substance?

Tick **one** box. [1 mark]

☐ A substance that is broken down by microbes.

☐ A substance that does not break down easily in water.

☐ A substance that harms or kills microorganisms in the soil.

4. Polymers can be disposed of in different ways.

The column on the left lists different methods of disposal.

The column on the right lists descriptions of disposal methods.

Draw **one** line from each method to the correct description.

We have done one to help you. [2 marks]

Method

Incineration

Landfill site

Recycling

Description

place where waste can be buried underground

chopping into small pieces for use as garden compost

burning waste at high temperatures

processing a material so it can be used again

5. The photograph shows different polymer objects collected at a recycling centre.

Give **two** reasons why recycling this polymer waste may be difficult.

_____

_____ [2 marks]

Mini test

1. The column on the left lists two separations.

The column on the right lists some methods of separation.

a Draw **one** line from each separation to the correct method of separation.

[2 marks]

Outcome 5

Description of separation

Glass from a mixture of glass and water

Pure water from ink

Method

crystallisation

distillation

filtration

b Use the correct answer from the box to complete the sentence. [1 mark]

Outcome 6

colours   distances   spots

In paper chromatography, a solvent carries compounds different

_____.

2. Marine aluminium is used in ship building.

The diagram shows the structure of this metal.

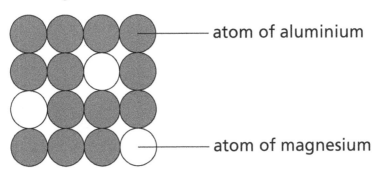

atom of aluminium

atom of magnesium

a Which state of matter does the diagram show? [1 mark]

Outcome 3

Draw a circle around the correct answer.

gas   liquid   solid

b Marine aluminium is a mixture of two metals.

What do we call this type of mixture? [1 mark]

Outcome 9

Tick **one** box.

☐ alloy   ☐ compound   ☐ polymer

c Marine aluminium has useful properties.

Use the correct answers from the box to complete
the sentences. [2 marks]

Outcomes 8 & 9

| conduction | corrosion | harder | softer |

Marine aluminium is used in ship building because it is _____
than pure aluminium.

It is not damaged by seawater because it is resistant to _____ .

3. There are about 100 different elements.

a What can we say about an element? [1 mark]

Outcome 1

Tick **one** box.

☐ It is made of only one sort of atom.

☐ It is made of two sorts of atom joined together.

☐ It is made of two sorts of atom mixed together.

b Part of the Periodic table is shown below.

Groups

1	2											3	4	5	6	7	0
					H												He
Li	Be											B	C	N	O	F	Ne
Na	Mg											Al	Si	P	S	Cl	Ar
K	Ca	Sc	Ti	V	Cr	Mn	Fe	Co	Ni	Cu	Zn	Ga	Ge	As	Se	Br	Kr

What can we say about the elements in the Periodic table?

[1 mark]
Outcome 1

Tick **one** box.

☐ About half of them are metals.

☐ Most of them are metals.

☐ Most of them are non-metals.

c Which two elements have similar chemical properties?

[1 mark]
Outcome 1

Draw **one** circle around the correct answer.

B and C   **F and Ne**   **H and Fe**   **Li and Na**

d Complete the word equation for the reaction between two non-metals to produce carbon dioxide.

_____ + _____ → carbon dioxide

[1 mark]
Outcome 2

4. Poly(propylene) is a polymer.

It is used to make bags, water pipes and garden chairs.

a Which of these is a property of poly(propylene)?

[1 mark]
Outcome 10

Tick **one** box.

☐ cannot be moulded   ☐ waterproof   ☐ weak

b Use the correct answers from the box to complete the sentences.

[2 marks]
Outcome 10

biodegradable   **landfill**   **microbes**   **recycle**

It is difficult to _____ polymers because there are many different types.

Polymers do not rot easily because they are not _____.

5. Diamond and graphite are forms of one element.

a Complete the sentence.   [1 mark]
Outcome 4

Diamond and graphite are forms of the element _____ .

b The column on the left lists some properties of diamond and graphite.

The column on the right lists two substances.

Draw **one** line from each property to the correct substance.   [3 marks]
Outcome 4

Property   **Substance**

| Hard |

| diamond |

| Slippery |

| graphite |

| Atoms arranged in layers |

6. We can extract metals from their ores.

a Iron ore contains iron oxide. What can we say about iron oxide?

[1 mark]
Outcome 7

Tick **one** box.

☐ It is a compound.   ☐ It is an element.   ☐ It is a mixture.

b The table show three metals and their reactivity.

Metal	Reactivity
Aluminium	More reactive than carbon
Platinum	Unreactive
Zinc	Less reactive than carbon

Which of these metals is extracted by heating its   [1 mark]
ore with carbon?   Outcome 7

_____

Total: 20 marks

Outcome 1: Acids and salts

- Acids react with some metals to make a salt and hydrogen gas.
- A word equation shows the reactants and the products.

acid + metal → salt + hydrogen gas

- Hydrochloric acid reacts with metals to make chlorides. Sulfuric acid reacts with metals to make sulfates.
- You can test if a gas is hydrogen by holding a burning splint at the end of an open test tube of the gas. The hydrogen burns and makes a squeaky pop sound.

1. Iron is a metal that reacts with acids to produce a salt.

   Complete the table by writing the name of the salt that is formed when iron reacts with each acid.

Acid used	Name of the iron salt produced
Hydrochloric acid	
Sulfuric acid	

   [2 marks]

2. Acids react with some metals to produce a salt and hydrogen gas.

   Use the correct answers from the box to complete the word equation.

chloride	hydrogen	sulfate

   Hydrochloric acid + zinc → zinc _____ + _____ [2 marks]

3. Magnesium reacts with acids to produce a salt and a gas.

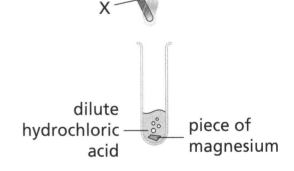

a What is the name of the piece of equipment marked as X on the diagram?

_____ [1 mark]

b What is the name of the gas produced in this reaction?

_____ [1 mark]

c What happens to the gas that is produced?

_____ [1 mark]

d What is the name of the salt that is produced in this reaction?

Tick **one** box.

☐ magnesium sulfate   ☐ zinc chloride

☐ magnesium chloride   ☐ zinc sulfate   [1 mark]

4.

GCSE Grade 1

Leah performs an experiment to measure the volume of hydrogen gas produced when three different metals are added to dilute hydrochloric acid. The metals used are magnesium, zinc and iron.

a Which are control variables for this experiment?

Tick **two** boxes.

Tip
Read all the possible answers before making your choices.

☐ Same volume of acid.

☐ Same concentration of acid.

☐ Same person doing the experiment.

☐ Same time for the experiment.   [2 marks]

b Which is the independent variable in this experiment?

_____ [1 mark]

Outcome 2: Neutralisation

- Neutralisation happens when an acid reacts with an alkali or a base. This makes a salt and water.

  acid + alkali → salt + water
  acid + insoluble base → salt + water

- Acids can also be neutralised by metal carbonates to produce a salt, water and carbon dioxide gas.

  acid + metal carbonate → salt + water + carbon dioxide

- To test if a gas is carbon dioxide bubble it through clear limewater. Carbon dioxide turns limewater milky.
- Crystallisation produces a solid salt from its solution.

1. Use the words from the box to complete the table.

| hydrochloric acid | magnesium oxide | potassium hydroxide | methane |

Acid	Alkali	Insoluble base

[3 marks]

2. Word equations can describe neutralisation reactions.

Complete the following word equations.   [5 marks]

hydrochloric acid + _____ → sodium chloride + _____

_____ + calcium oxide → calcium sulfate + water

zinc carbonate + sulfuric acid → _____ + _____ + water

3. Salt crystals used on food can be extracted from seawater.

Use the words from the box to complete the sentences.

| crystallisation | crystals | distillation | solution |

_____ can be produced from a _____ of sodium chloride,

by the process of _____.   [3 marks]

4.

GCSE Grade 1

The diagram shows the apparatus used to test the gas produced during the neutralisation reaction of hydrochloric acid and copper carbonate powder.

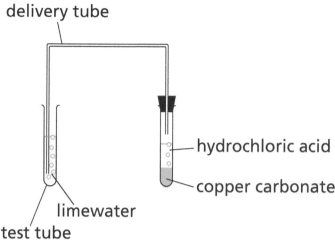

delivery tube

hydrochloric acid

copper carbonate

limewater

test tube

a   Name the gas produced during this reaction.

_____ [1 mark]

b   Complete the word equation for this reaction.

copper carbonate + hydrochloric acid → copper _____ +

_____ + water   [2 marks]

c   During the gas test, the gas is bubbled through limewater.

Complete the sentence.

_____ gas turns limewater from clear

to _____.   [2 marks]

d   The experiment is repeated with copper chloride powder instead of copper carbonate.

What would you expect to happen?

Tick **one** box.

☐   No visible reaction.

☐   Bubbles of gas are produced that turn the limewater milky white.

☐   Bubbles of gas are produced that do not turn the limewater milky white.

☐   The green copper chloride powder turns black.   [1 mark]

Outcome 3: Energy transfers in chemistry

- Reactions such as combustion, oxidation and neutralisation transfer energy to the surroundings.
- Reactions such as dissolving ammonium chloride in water take in energy from the surroundings. This causes the temperature to decrease.

. . . .

1.   During a chemical reaction, the temperature can:

A   stay the same

B   increase

C   decrease

For each of the following reactions write the **correct letter** (A, B, or C) in the box, describing the temperature change that will occur.

burning magnesium in air   ☐

mixing sugar solution and salt solution   ☐

neutralising hydrochloric acid with sodium hydroxide ☐

dissolving ammonium chloride in water   ☐   [4 marks]

2.   The table below shows the results of four chemical reactions. In each, a solid powder, A, B, C or D, was added to water.

The temperature of the water was measured before and after the solid powders were added.

Meera wanted to find out if energy was transferred in or out by the reaction. For **each** reaction, tick the correct box in the table.   [4 marks]

Powder	Temperature of the water (°C)		Energy is transferred in	Energy is transferred out
	Before	**After**		
A	20	15		
B	21	32		
C	19	27		
D	19	12		

3. Josh performed an experiment to measure the temperature change during chemical reactions. He used:

GCSE Grade 1

- 5 cm³ sulfuric acid

- 0.5 g samples of metal oxides.

He measured the temperature before the reaction and the temperature after the reaction.

His results are shown in the table.

Metal oxide sample	Temperature before the reaction (°C)	Temperature after the reaction (°C)	Temperature change (°C)
Zinc oxide	20	28	8
Iron oxide	20	32	
Magnesium oxide	20	39	

a Complete the table by calculating the temperature change of the reactions.

We have done one to help you. [2 marks]

b Complete the bar chart of the results.

We have done zinc oxide for you.

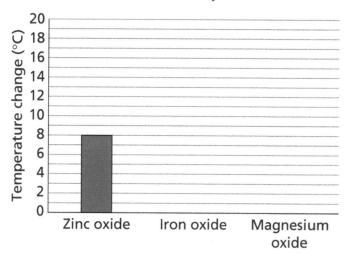

Tip
The bars on a bar chart should all be the same width.

[3 marks]

c Select the name of the variable that the student was changing.

Tick **one** box

☐ Mass of the metal oxides.

☐ Type of the metal oxide.

☐ Temperature change of the reaction. [1 mark]

Outcome 4: Rate of reaction

- The rate of a chemical reaction can be increased by:
  - increasing the temperature
  - increasing the concentration of reactants
  - increasing the surface area of solid reactants
  - adding a suitable catalyst.
- The rate of a chemical reaction may be measured by:
  - the time taken for the reactants to be used up
  - the volume of a gas produced in a set time
  - the time taken for a solution to become coloured or opaque.

1. A magnesium metal strip reacts with dilute hydrochloric acid to produce hydrogen gas. The magnesium strip is used up during the reaction.

   Which changes will increase the rate of the reaction?

   Tick **three** boxes.

   ☐ Increase the temperature of the hydrochloric acid.

   ☐ Add more water to the hydrochloric acid.

   ☐ Use more concentrated hydrochloric acid.

   ☐ Use magnesium powder instead of magnesium strip.   [3 marks]

2. Daisy put a magnesium strip in hydrochloric acid.

   Every 20 seconds for 100 seconds, she measured the volume of hydrogen gas produced using a gas syringe.

   She did the experiment at 20 °C and 50 °C.

   In both experiments she used the same volume and concentration of acid and the same length of magnesium strip.

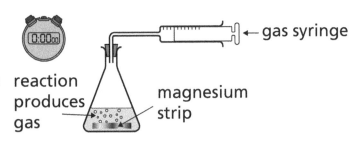

The results are shown in the graph.

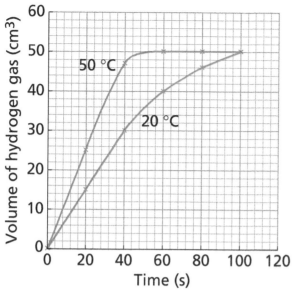

a Use the graph to find the volume of hydrogen gas produced after 60 s.

At 20 °C: _____ cm³

At 50 °C: _____ cm³ [2 marks]

b At each temperature, the final volume of hydrogen gas produced was 50 cm³.

What is the best explanation for this?

Tick **one** box.

☐ The temperature was different in each experiment.

☐ The volume of gas increased in both experiments.

☐ The length of magnesium strip was the same in both experiments. [1 mark]

GCSE Grade 1 **c** At which temperature was the rate of reaction fastest?

Tick **one** box.

☐ 20 °C   ☐ 50 °C [1 mark]

d How can you tell this from the graph?

_____ [1 mark]

Outcome 5: The early atmosphere

- In the early atmosphere of the Earth, volcanoes released gases and water vapour.
  - o The gases formed the first atmosphere.
  - o The water vapour condensed to form the first oceans.
- When algae and plants evolved there was little or no oxygen.
- About three billion years ago, algae and plants evolved. They produced oxygen by the process of photosynthesis.

1. The pie chart shows the percentage of gases in the early atmosphere.

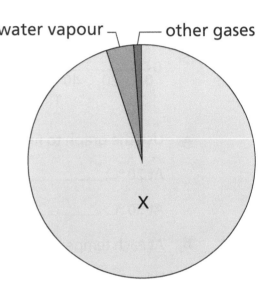

water vapour — — other gases

X

a Name gas X. _____

[1 mark]

b Where did the gases of the early atmosphere come from?

_____ [1 mark]

c Use the correct answers from the box to complete the sentence.

atmosphere condensed evaporated volcanoes water vapour

The early _____ contained _____ that

_____ to form the early oceans. [3 marks]

2. The Earth's atmosphere formed over billions of years.

a Which organisms produced oxygen that went into the early atmosphere?

Tick **one** box.

☐ plants and animals

☐ plants and algae [1 mark]

b What is the process that produced the oxygen found in the early atmosphere?

Tick **one** box.

☐ combustion

☐ photosynthesis [1 mark]

c Which word equation shows the process that produced oxygen in the early atmosphere?

Tick **one** box.

☐ oxygen + carbon dioxide → glucose + water

☐ carbon dioxide + water → glucose + oxygen

☐ water + glucose → carbon dioxide + oxygen [1 mark]

3.

Some scientists compare the early atmosphere of Earth to the atmosphere of the planet Mars today.

The pie chart shows the percentage of gases in the current atmosphere of Mars.

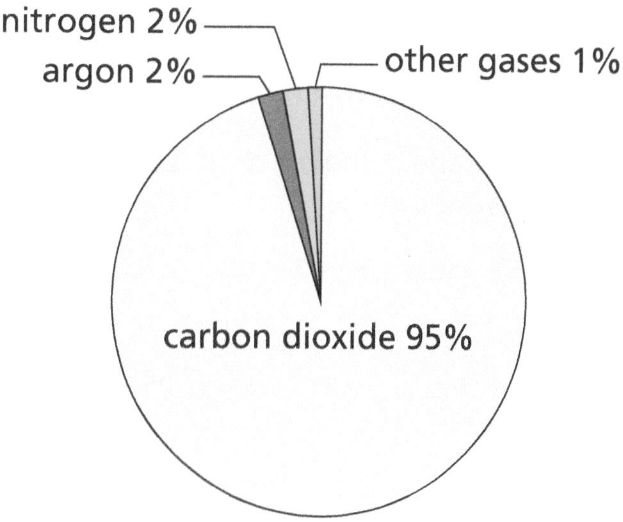

Why do some scientists think that the atmosphere of Mars is similar to the early atmosphere of Earth?

Tick **one** box.

☐ The atmosphere of Mars contains argon.

☐ The atmosphere of Mars contains a similar percentage of carbon dioxide as the early atmosphere of Earth.

☐ The atmosphere of Mars does not contain water vapour.

☐ The atmosphere of Mars contains a similar percentage of nitrogen as the early atmosphere of Earth. [1 mark]

nitrogen 2%

argon 2%

other gases 1%

carbon dioxide 95%

Outcome 6: The atmosphere today

- Plants and algae removed some of the carbon dioxide in the early atmosphere by photosynthesis. Some carbon dioxide dissolved in the oceans.
- Much of the carbon contained in the carbon dioxide is now locked up in rocks.
- The modern atmosphere consists of about 80% nitrogen and about 20% oxygen. There are also small amounts of gases such as carbon dioxide, water vapour and argon.

1.   The Earth's atmosphere has changed over time.

Use the correct answers from the box to complete the sentences.

atmosphere   carbon dioxide   dissolved   oceans   photosynthesis

The early atmosphere contained mostly _____ gas.

_____ by plants and algae removed some of this gas from the atmosphere.

Some of the gas also _____ in the _____ .   [4 marks]

2.   The modern atmosphere contains about 80% nitrogen and 20% oxygen.

Shade in the pie chart. **Label** each area to show the composition of the modern atmosphere.

Each segment is 10% of the total.

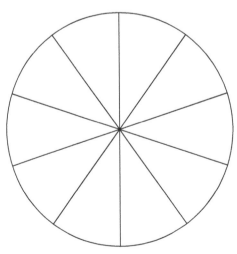

[3 marks]

3. Some of the carbon contained within the carbon dioxide gas is now locked up in the Earth. How has this occurred?

Tick **two** boxes.

☐ It has been converted into coal, oil and gas.

☐ It is frozen in ice sheets.

☐ It has been converted into carbonate rocks.

☐ It has been converted into molten rock. [2 marks]

4.

Jack used a gas sensor to measure the percentage of different gases in fresh air and exhaled air (the air that we breathe out). His results are shown in the table.

a Work out the percentage of oxygen in exhaled air.

Write your answer in the table. [1 mark]

Gas	Fresh air	Exhaled air
Nitrogen	80%	80%
Oxygen	19%	%
Carbon dioxide	1%	4%

b Why are the percentages of oxygen and carbon dioxide in fresh air and exhaled air different?

Tick **one** box.

☐ Respiration uses up carbon dioxide and releases oxygen.

☐ Respiration uses up oxygen and releases carbon dioxide.

☐ Photosynthesis uses up carbon dioxide and releases oxygen.

☐ Photosynthesis uses up oxygen and releases carbon dioxide. [1 mark]

c Which gas remains unchanged during breathing?

Tick **one** box.

☐ water vapour   ☐ oxygen

☐ carbon dioxide   ☐ nitrogen   [1 mark]

Outcome 7: Crude oil

- Crude oil is found underground in oil fields.
- Crude oil is a mixture of many compounds.
- Crude oil is separated into fractions by fractional distillation.
- Fractions are useful parts of crude oil that can be used as fuels and oils. These include petrol and diesel.

1. What type of substance is crude oil?

Tick **one** box.

☐ solid ☐ gas ☐ mixture

☐ compound ☐ fraction [1 mark]

2. Use the correct answers from the box to complete the sentences about crude oil.

fractions	mixture	petrol	refinery	useful

Crude oil is separated into _____ in a _____.

Fractions are _____ products of fractional distillation. They include

_____ and diesel. [4 marks]

3. The diagram shows the fractions separated from crude oil.

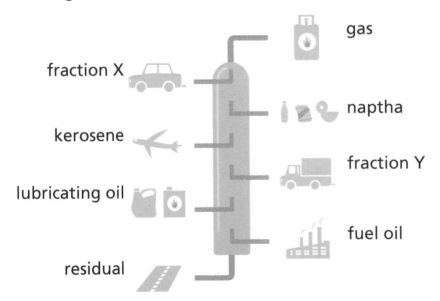

a What is this process called?

Tick **one** box.

☐ chromatography

☐ filtration

☐ fractional distillation [1 mark]

b Name these **two** fractions from the diagram.

Fraction X is _____ .

Fraction Y is _____ . [2 marks]

c Kerosene is a useful fraction of crude oil. What is kerosene used for?

Tick **one** box.

☐ road surfacing

☐ lubricating moving parts of an engine

☐ aircraft fuel

☐ heating buildings [1 mark]

4.

GCSE Grade 1

During fractional distillation, crude oil is heated at the bottom of the fractional distillation column. The different fractions have different boiling points. Bitumen has the highest boiling point.

a Which fraction of crude oil has the lowest boiling point?

Use the diagram in question 3 to help you.

_____ [1 mark]

b How does the temperature change inside the fractional distillation column?

_____

_____ [2 marks]

Outcome 8: Burning fuels

- Complete burning happens when fuels burn with lots of oxygen.
- The gases that are released include carbon dioxide, water vapour and oxides of nitrogen.
- If there is limited oxygen when a fuel burns, the combustion is incomplete. Carbon monoxide gas and solid particles of soot may be produced.
- Carbon monoxide is a colourless, odourless, poisonous gas, which can cause death.
- Burning fossil fuels affects the environment.
  - o Acid rain forms when sulfur dioxide and oxides of nitrogen dissolve in rain water. Acid rain can damage tree leaves and kill fish in lakes.
  - o Solid soot particles cause global dimming. This can cause photosynthesis to slow down.

1. Use the correct answers from the box to complete the sentences. [5 marks]

combustion	complete	fuel	limited	oxygen	sulfur

_____ combustion occurs when a _____ burns with

plenty of _____ .

Incomplete _____ occurs when there is _____ oxygen.

2. Which gases can be formed when a fuel, such as coal, burns completely?

Tick **three** boxes.

☐ carbon dioxide

☐ nitrogen

☐ water vapour

☐ sulfur dioxide

☐ argon [3 marks]

3. Why is incomplete combustion dangerous to humans?

Tick **one** box.

☐ A lot of heat is produced.

☐ Carbon dioxide is produced, which is a poisonous gas.

☐ Carbon monoxide is produced, which is a poisonous gas.

☐ Water vapour is produced.   [1 mark]

4. Burning fuel can harm the environment.

The column on the left lists some pollutants.

The column of the right lists some harmful effects on the environment.

Draw **one** line from each pollutant to its harmful effect.

Pollutants   **Harmful effect**

soil erosion

Sulfur dioxide

global dimming

Solid soot particles

acid rain   [2 marks]

5. Carbon monoxide is a poisonous gas.

It is formed when fuels burn without enough oxygen.

Give **two** reasons why it is difficult for humans to detect carbon monoxide.

1. _____

2. _____   [2 marks]

6. Give **two** reasons why using wind turbines instead of burning fossil fuels to generate electricity can reduce harmful effects on the environment.

GCSE Grade 1

1. _____

2. _____   [2 marks]

Outcome 9: Greenhouse gases

- Carbon dioxide and methane are greenhouse gases. Human activities increase the level of these gases in the atmosphere.
  o Burning fossil fuels increase the amount of carbon dioxide.
  o Landfill and cattle farming increase the amount of methane.
- The temperature of the atmosphere increases as the level of greenhouse gases increases. Most scientists believe that this is causing global climate change.

1. Which gases are greenhouse gases?

   Tick **two** boxes.

   ☐ argon   ☐ methane   ☐ nitrogen   ☐ carbon dioxide   [2 marks]

2. Which human activities are linked to global climate change?

   Tick **three** boxes.

   ☐ cattle farming

   ☐ using solar power

   ☐ burning coal

   ☐ putting food waste in landfill

   ☐ insulating houses   [3 marks]

3. Greenhouse gases have been linked to global climate change.

   a Many people argue about the link between increased greenhouse gases and global warming. Which of the following statements are true?

   Tick **two** boxes.

   ☐ All scientists agree about the link.

   ☐ Many scientists agree about the link.

   ☐ Some scientists do not agree about the link.   [2 marks]

b Which of the following are possible results of global warming?

Tick **two** boxes.

☐ rising sea levels

☐ increased burning of fossil fuels

☐ greater risk of droughts

☐ greater human population [2 marks]

4.

GCSE Grade 1

The graph shows changes in global temperature and the amount of carbon dioxide in the atmosphere in the last 1000 years.

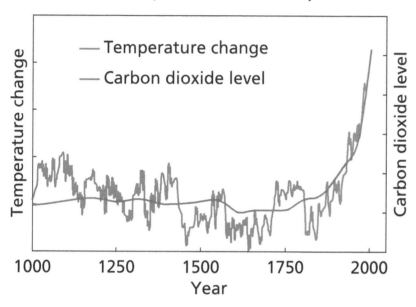

Tick **one** box on **each row** of the table to correctly complete each sentence. [3 marks]

	increased	stayed about the same	decreased
Between the years 1000 and 1500, the level of carbon dioxide			
Between the years 1750 and 2000, the temperature change			
Between the years 1750 and 2000, the level of carbon dioxide			

Outcome 10: Water for drinking

- Safe drinking water contains small amounts of dissolved substances and few microbes.
- Most safe drinking water comes from fresh water sources. It is sterilised using ultraviolet light to kill microbes and filtered to remove solids.
- Salty water can be distilled to make fresh water. This method requires a large energy input.

1. Use the correct answers from the box to complete the sentence about safe drinking water.

dissolved	large	microbes	small	solids

Safe drinking water contains _____ amounts of _____

substances and very low levels of _____.   [3 marks]

2. Suggest a way to remove solid particles from fresh water.

_____   [1 mark]

3. Why is drinking water sterilised?

_____ [1 mark]

4. In the UK what are the main sources of safe drinking water?

Tick **two** boxes

☐ lakes   ☐ sewers and drains   ☐ rivers   [2 marks]

5. The diagram shows a method of making seawater drinkable.

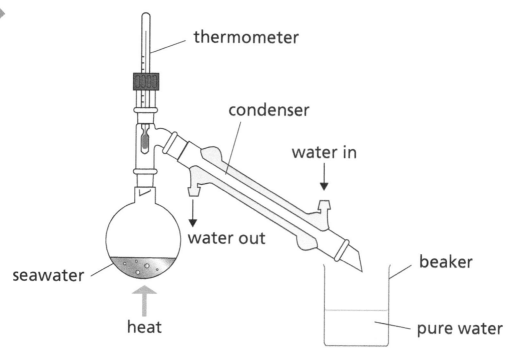

a Suggest a heat source for this apparatus in the laboratory.

_____ [1 mark]

b Name this process.

Tick **one** box.

☐ filtration   ☐ distillation

☐ condensation   ☐ chromatography   [1 mark]

c Very little drinking water in the UK is produced from seawater. One reason is because we have a lot of fresh water.

What is another reason why seawater is not used to produce drinking water in the UK?

_____ [1 mark]

Mini test

1. The pie charts show the gases in Earth's early atmosphere and the current atmosphere.

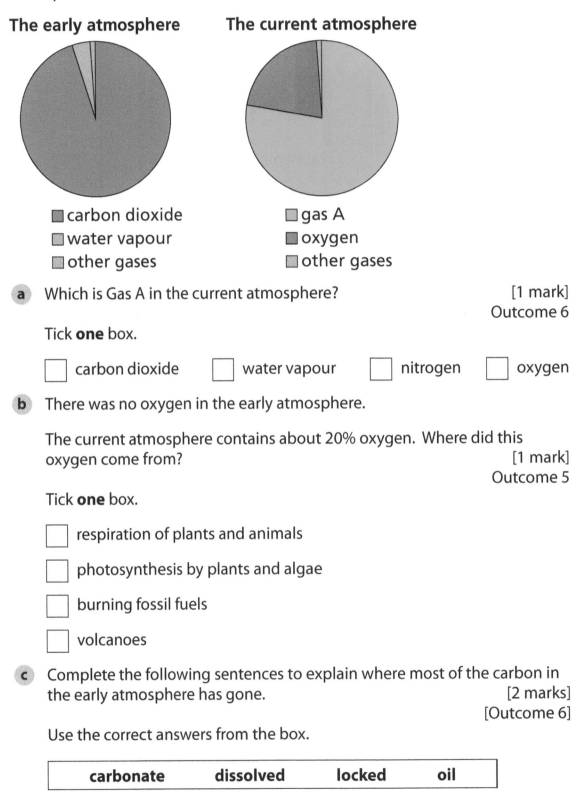

The early atmosphere   **The current atmosphere**

- ■ carbon dioxide   ■ gas A
- ■ water vapour   ■ oxygen
- ■ other gases   ■ other gases

a Which is Gas A in the current atmosphere?   [1 mark]
Outcome 6

Tick **one** box.

☐ carbon dioxide   ☐ water vapour   ☐ nitrogen   ☐ oxygen

b There was no oxygen in the early atmosphere.

The current atmosphere contains about 20% oxygen. Where did this oxygen come from?   [1 mark]
Outcome 5

Tick **one** box.

☐ respiration of plants and animals

☐ photosynthesis by plants and algae

☐ burning fossil fuels

☐ volcanoes

c Complete the following sentences to explain where most of the carbon in the early atmosphere has gone.   [2 marks]
[Outcome 6]

Use the correct answers from the box.

| carbonate | dissolved | locked | oil |

Most of the carbon that was contained in the carbon dioxide of the

early atmosphere has now been _____ up in the Earth's rocks.

Some has been changed into _____ rocks and some has been
changed into fossil fuels.

2. Acids react with alkalis producing a salt and water.

a What is the name of this process? [1 mark]
Outcome 2

_____

b Sulfuric acid and potassium hydroxide react in this way.

Which is the word equation for this reaction? [1 mark]
Outcome 2

Tick **one** box.

☐ sulfuric acid + potassium hydroxide → potassium chloride + water

☐ sulfuric acid + potassium hydroxide → potassium sulfate + hydrogen

☐ sulfuric acid + potassium hydroxide → potassium sulfate + water

c When an acid reacts with a metal such as magnesium, hydrogen gas is
produced. What is the test for hydrogen gas? [1 mark]
Outcome 1

Tick **one** box.

☐ A burning splint stops burning.

☐ A glowing splint starts to burn.

☐ The gas turns limewater milky white.

☐ A burning splint burns quickly with a squeaky pop sound.

3. Dirty water must be treated before it is safe
to drink. A method to do this on a small scale
in the laboratory is shown in the diagram.

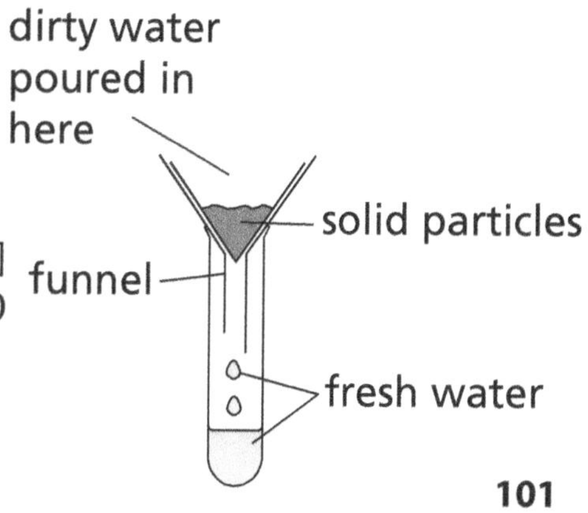

dirty water
poured in
here

a What is the name of this
process?
[1 mark]
Outcome 10

solid particles

funnel

fresh water

_____

b The fresh water produced by this method is still not safe to drink.
Select a possible reason for this. [1 mark]

Outcome 10

Tick **one** box.

☐ The fresh water needs to be sterilised to kill any microbes.

☐ The fresh water needs to be neutralised.

☐ The fresh water needs to be stored to let any particles settle.

4. Crude oil needs to be processed in a refinery before it can be used.

a Complete the sentence about crude oil. [2 marks]

Outcome 7

Use the correct answers from the box.

elements	fractions	mixture	solution

Crude oil is a _____ of different useful _____.

b Name the process that separates crude oil into its useful fractions. [1 mark]

Outcome 7

_____

c When petrol and diesel are burned in a car engine, gases are released that can harm the environment.

The column on the left lists some harmful effects on the environment.

The column on the right lists some gases.

Draw one line from each harmful effect to a gas. [2 marks]

Outcome 8 and 9

Harmful effect   **Gas**

carbon dioxide

Acid rain   nitrogen

Global warming   sulfur dioxide

hydrogen

5. When some reactions occur there is a change in the temperature of the reacting substances.

For each reaction in the table tick the correct box. [2 marks]
Outcome 3

Reaction	The temperature **increases**	The temperature **decreases**
Combustion of methane gas		
Dissolving ammonium chloride in water		

6. Calcium carbonate is a white compound. It reacts with colourless sulfuric acid and forms a colourless solution of the salt called calcium sulfate, as well as water and carbon dioxide gas.

a Which of the following ways could the rate of reaction be measured? [2 marks]
Outcome 4

Tick **two** boxes.

☐ Measuring the mass of the calcium carbonate before and after the reaction.

☐ Measuring the temperature before and after the reaction.

☐ Measuring the time taken to produce 10 cm^3 samples of the carbon dioxide gas.

☐ Measuring the time taken for the white compound to completely disappear.

b Write down **two** ways that the rate of this reaction could be increased. [2 marks]
Outcome 4

1. _____

2. _____

Total: 20 marks

PHYSICS

Outcome 1: Energy changes

- An object can have different stores of energy.
  - o A train has a store of kinetic energy when it is moving.
  - o An oven has a store of thermal energy when it is hot.
  - o A person at the top of a tower has a store of gravitational potential energy.
  - o A spring has a store of elastic energy when it is squashed.
- Energy can move between the different stores, but the total amount of energy stays the same. Energy is never lost, but it can be dissipated (spread around) to less useful stores.

1. Which statement about an electric kettle heating up is true?

Tick **one** box.

☐ The store of thermal energy in the kettle decreases.

☐ The kettle's store of gravitational potential energy increases.

☐ The kettle's store of thermal energy increases. [1 mark]

2. The column on the left lists a description of an apple.

The column on the right lists some energy stores

Draw **one** line from each description to the energy store it matches.

Description	Energy store
An apple hanging in a tree	thermal
An apple that has been thrown	kinetic
An apple in the oven	gravitational potential

[3 marks]

3. A rollercoaster speeds up as it travels down a track.

Use the correct answers from the box to complete each sentence.

You can use each answer more than once.

down	faster	up

The store of gravitational potential energy of the rollercoaster goes

_____.

The store of kinetic energy of the rollercoaster goes _____.

A small amount of the energy is dissipated to thermal energy stores because of friction between the wheels and the track. The temperature of wheels goes

_____.   [3 marks]

4.   A cyclist brakes hard and comes to a stop.

The store of kinetic energy of the bicycle goes down. Where has most of the energy gone?

Tick **one** box.

☐ The brakes have more thermal energy.

☐ The air around the cyclist has more elastic energy.

☐ The bicycle has more gravitational potential energy.   [1 mark]

5.   Alison fires a catapult.

GCSE Grade 1

Use the correct answer from the box to complete each sentence.

| elastic | gravitational potential | kinetic | thermal |

As Alison pulls back a catapult, the rubber straps increase their store of

_____ energy.

When she lets go of the catapult the stone is flying very fast. It has increased its

store of _____ energy.

The stone slows down as it flies higher. It increases its store of _____ energy.   [3 marks]

Outcome 2: Energy transfers

- Energy can be transferred between energy stores, but it cannot be created or destroyed.
- A more efficient system transfers more of the input energy into useful forms of energy.
- A less efficient system dissipates (wastes) more of the input energy into non-useful forms of energy.
- By lubricating (oiling) moving parts and insulating between objects we can reduce the dissipated energy.
- If a wall has a high thermal conductivity heat passes quickly through it.

1. The column on the left lists some words.

   The column on the right lists some definitions.

   Draw **one** line from each word to its definition.

Word	Definition
Absorber	an object that is giving out energy
Emitter	transfer of thermal energy as a wave
Radiation	an object that is taking in energy

   [3 marks]

2. Dishwasher A uses 1.5 kWh of energy to wash its dishes.

   Dishwasher B uses 2 kWh of energy to do the same thing.

   Use the correct answer from the box to complete the sentence.

more effective	**less effective**	**more efficient**	**less efficient**

   Dishwasher A is _____. [1 mark]

3. The Greek island of Santorini is hotter than the UK, and so their buildings look different.

   a The buildings are painted white to keep them cool in summer.

   How does the colour of a wall affect what happens to radiation from the sun hitting it?

Tick **one** box.

☐ Light walls reflect more radiation.

☐ Dark walls reflect more radiation. [1 mark]

b Buildings in Greece have very thick walls to help the buildings maintain a constant temperature.

Use the correct answers from the box to complete the sentences.

| conductors | decrease | higher | increase | insulators | lower |

Thick walls are better _____ than thin walls.

This is because they have a _____ thermal conductivity.

Thick walls _____ the rate at which thermal energy is dissipated. [3 marks]

4. An insulated flask for keeping drinks hot or cold is made from two layers of stainless steel with a narrow gap in between them.

GCSE Grade 1

stainless steel

gap

Which are the correct statements about the design of a flask?

Tick **two** boxes.

☐ There is no air in the gap of the flask, to reduce heat conduction.

☐ There is a lot of air in the gap of the flask, to reduce heat insulation.

☐ The walls of the flask are polished and shiny to reflect radiation.

☐ The walls of the flask are matt and dull to absorb radiation. [2 marks]

Outcome 3: Energy resources

- Some energy resources are non-renewable because they will run out. Examples are coal, oil, gas and nuclear fuel.
- Some energy resources are renewable because they do not run out. Examples are bio-fuel, wind, hydroelectricity, geothermal, tides, sun and water waves.
- Most power stations have a turbine that spins. The turbine then turns a generator to create electricity.
- Solar cells can generate electricity directly from the Sun's radiation.

1. One source of bio-fuel is sugarcane, which can be used to make ethanol.

This can then be used to power cars.

Which of the following is a big advantage of bio-fuels over petrol?

Tick **one** box.

☐ Bio-fuels are free.

☐ Bio-fuels can make the car go further.

☐ Bio-fuels are a renewable energy resource. [1 mark]

2. Which of the following are non-renewable ways of generating electricity?

Tick **two** boxes.

☐ geothermal power stations

☐ oil power stations

☐ nuclear power stations

☐ tidal power stations

☐ solar cells [2 marks]

3. Fossil fuel power stations, such as coal power stations, burn the fuel to create steam in a boiler.

This steam spins a turbine.

The turbine then turns a generator to create electricity.

Use **two** correct answers from the box to label the diagram of a power station.

boiler	generator	turbine	transformer

fuel

grid

[2 marks]

4. There is a lot of debate about nuclear power stations.

They use uranium to generate electricity.

For each statement tick whether it is an advantage or a disadvantage of nuclear power.

Argument	Advantage	Disadvantage
The uranium remains radioactive for thousands of years.		
Nuclear power uses less fuel to create the same energy as coal.		
Less greenhouse gases are given off by nuclear power stations than by fossil fuel power stations.		

[3 marks]

5. This is a mixed-up list to describe how a tidal power station works.

GCSE Grade 1 Number the sentences in the order they happen.

We have done one to help you.

When the tide goes in or out it makes the water move quickly forwards or backwards. `1`

This turns an electrical generator. ☐

The turbine blades in the water spin around. ☐

Electricity is then taken back to shore by cables on the sea floor. ☐

[3 marks]

Outcome 4: Contact and non-contact forces

- A force is a push or pull acting on an object.
- A contact-force acts between two objects that are touching. Examples are air resistance, friction and tension.
- Some forces can act between objects without them needing to touch. Examples of these non-contact forces include magnetic, electrostatic (between two charged objects) and gravitational forces.
- When an object rests on a surface it feels a normal contact force pushing up and this balances the weight.

1. What force causes an object to feel weighty?

    Draw a circle around the correct answer.

    magnetic   **electrostatic**   **gravitational**

    [1 mark]

2. A dumper truck is parked.

    Use the correct answers from the box to label the forces acting on the dumper truck.

air resistance	normal contact force	pressure	weight

    [2 marks]

3. Brian is pushing a shopping trolley.

Use the correct answers from the box to complete the sentences.

friction	force	mass	power	weight

When Brian is pushing the trolley, he applies a _____ to push it forwards.

He then releases the trolley and it slowly rolls to a stop.

_____ causes the trolley to slow down. [2 marks]

4. A parachutist jumps out of a plane.

As she moves faster, which force increases?

Draw a circle around the correct answer.

air resistance   **gravitational**   **kinetic**

[1 mark]

5. The column on the left lists a description of some movements.

GCSE Grade 1

The column on the right lists some forces.

Draw **one** line from each description to the force that causes it.

Description   **Force**

| An electron moving around the nucleus. | | tension |

| A conker spinning around on a string. | | gravitational |

| The Earth orbiting the sun. | | electrostatic | [3 marks]

Outcome 5: Work

- When a force causes an object to move, work is done by the force.
- When work is done against friction, it causes the object to get hotter.
- Sometimes when friction causes heat it can be useful, such as lighting a match.
- Sometimes when friction causes heat it is not helpful. For example, when a drill gets very hot.

1. Which sentence best describes why rubbing your hands together on a cold winter's day warms them up?

   Tick **one** box.

   ☐ It makes them closer so they lose less heat.

   ☐ They are better insulated when moving quickly.

   ☐ The friction between the hands heats them up.   [1 mark]

2. The column on the left lists some words.

   The column on the right lists some definitions.

   Draw **one** line from each word to its definition.

Word	Definition
Work	a contact force that tries to slow down a moving object
Force	a push or a pull, measured in newtons
Friction	how much energy is transferred when a force moves an object, measured in joules

   [3 marks]

3. Before he oiled his brother's pushchair, Harry found it difficult to push. Once the axles were lubricated he found it much easier to push.

   What decreased because he lubricated it?

   Draw a circle around the **two** correct answers.

   Brian's strength   pushing force   weight   work done   [2 marks]

4. Why are the disc brakes of a car open to the air?

Tick **one** box.

☐ Because they look better.

☐ To make them quicker to change.

☐ To stop them going rusty.

☐ So that they are cooled by the air passing them.   [1 mark]

5. Niloufar climbs a 3-metre ladder. She uses 1500 joules of energy.

GCSE Grade 1

Use the correct answers from the box to complete the sentences.

3000 joules	**4000 joules**	**force**
height	**weight**	**work**

As she climbs, she is doing _____ against gravity.

Alan now climbs the same ladder, but he uses 2500

joules. This is because his _____ is more.

Now Niloufar climbs a 6-metre ladder. She uses _____ of
energy to climb it.   [3 marks]

Outcome 6: Speed

- The speed of an object is the distance it travels in a certain amount of time.
- The equation $\text{speed} = \dfrac{\text{distance}}{\text{time}}$ can be used to calculate speed.
- Speed is often measured in metres per second (m/s), miles per hour (mph) and kilometres per hour (km/h)

1. How fast is this car going in kilometres per hour?

Tick **one** box.

☐ 60 kilometres per hour

☐ 87 kilometres per hour

☐ 96 kilometres per hour   [1 mark]

2. Your satellite navigation system says it will take you 3 hours to travel 180 miles.

The satellite navigation system assumes you will travel at an average speed. Use the equation to work out what your average speed would be.

$$\text{speed} = \frac{\text{distance}}{\text{time}}$$

_____

_____

Average speed = _____ miles per hour.   [2 marks]

3. Oscar the cat has a top speed of 30 km/h.

A dog called Harrison has a top speed of 25 km/h.

If they run the same distance who takes the shortest amount of time?

Draw a circle around the correct answer.

Oscar   **Harrison**   **both the same**

[1 mark]

4. Xena travels 60 km in 2 hours.

Yumi travels 35 km in 1 hour.

Zoe travels 90 km in 3 hours.

Use the equation below to work out the average speeds for these journeys.

$$\text{speed} = \frac{\text{distance}}{\text{time}}$$

Draw a circle around the correct answers.

a Who travels furthest?

    Xena   **Yumi**   **Zoe**   [1 mark]

b Who has travelled fastest?

    Xena   **Yumi**   **Zoe**   [1 mark]

5. Ewan runs 200 metres in 50 seconds.

GCSE Grade 1

Rory runs 500 metres in 100 seconds.

Complete the table.

Ewan's speed		m/s
Rory's speed		m/s
Difference in speed		m/s

[3 marks]

117

Outcome 7: Stopping distances

- The distance a car travels from when the driver sees an event to when the car comes to a stop is called the stopping distance.
- The distance the car travels during the driver's reaction time is called the thinking distance.
- The distance the car travels once the brakes have been pressed is called the braking distance.
- The stopping distance is the total of the thinking distance + braking distance.
- Driving faster increases the braking distance (unless the braking force changes as well).

1. What will increase when a car travels faster?

Draw a circle around the correct answer.

braking distance   **thinking distance**   **both**   [1 mark]

2. This diagram is from the Highway Code.

Source: 2018 edition of The Official Highway Code, Crown Copyright.

a What is the stopping distance of a car travelling at 30 mph?

_____   [1 mark]

b How much further is the braking distance of a car travelling at 60 mph compared to a car travelling at 30 mph?

Draw a circle around the correct answer.

double   **four times**   **the same**   [1 mark]

3. A driver tries to stop their car as quickly as possible.

If the braking force increases what happens to the thinking and braking distances?

a The thinking distance

Tick **one** box.

☐ decreases

☐ increases

☐ does not change

[1 mark]

b The braking distance

Tick **one** box.

☐ decreases

☐ increases

☐ does not change

[1 mark]

4. Complete the **three** blank spaces in this section of the Highway Code.

GCSE Grade 1

20 mph 6 ⟩ 6 ⟩ = 12 metres

Thinking distance

Braking distance

40 mph 12 m ⟩ ___m ⟩ = 36 metres

50 mph 15 m ⟩ 38 m ⟩ = ___ metres

70 mph ___m ⟩ 75 m ⟩ = 96 metres

Source: 2018 edition of The Official Highway Code, Crown Copyright.

[3 marks]

Outcome 8: Reaction times

- Reaction times for humans vary from about 0.2 seconds to 0.9 seconds. They can be measured in different ways.
- Reaction times can increase with the use of alcohol or drugs, as well as tiredness.
- Distractions can affect a driver's ability to react quickly.

1. Hassan and Isabel do an experiment to test Hassan's reaction times.

Isabel drops the ruler and Hassan catches it as quickly as he can.

The distance the ruler travels before Hassan catches it is related to his reaction times.

They repeat the experiment five times.

Draw a circle around the result that looks like an anomaly (looks odd or strange).

29 cm   **27 cm**   **29 cm**   **21 cm**   **30 cm**

[1 mark]

2. Hassan and Isabel repeat the experiment. This time Hassan repeats his times tables out loud while they do the experiment.

This time his results are:

41 cm   35 cm   39 cm   38 cm   42 cm

Which of the following statements is true?

Use the correct answer from the box to complete the sentence.

increased	decreased	stayed the same

When distracted, Hassan's reaction times _____.   [1 mark]

3. In England and Wales, the alcohol limit for drivers is 80 milligrams of alcohol per 100 millilitres of blood.

Why do we limit the amount of alcohol that drivers can safely drink?

Tick **two** boxes.

☐ It decreases reaction times.

☐ It increases reaction times.

☐ Drunk drivers make worse decisions.

☐ It increases braking distance. [2 marks]

4. Oona and Elijah tested their reaction times using a computer.

When the screen changed colour, they had to press a button using the index (first) finger from either their left or right hand. They are both right-handed.

This is the table of their results:

	Finger on left hand	Finger on right hand
Oona	0.33 s	0.28 s
Elijah	0.36 s	0.27 s

Use the correct words from the box below to complete the sentences.

always	**faster**	**never**	**slower**	**sometimes**

Oona was _____ faster than Elijah.

Using the left hand was _____ than using the right hand. [2 marks]

5. Rosa is driving a car when a bus suddenly pulls out in front of her. She brakes as quickly as possible.

What could increase the thinking distance?

Tick **three** boxes.

☐ Rosa is tired.

☐ The tyres on Rosa's car are worn.

☐ Rosa has been drinking alcohol.

☐ There are young children in the back being silly.

☐ The road is wet. [3 marks]

Outcome 9: Braking distance

- Road surfaces such as gravel, ice, water or leaves can increase the braking distance of a car.
- The braking distance of a car increases if the tyres or brakes are worn out.
- The tread (grooves) in a tyre is designed to get rid of water between the tyre and the road.
- Driving faster increases the braking distance of a car.

1. **a** A car manufacturer does a set of experiments to measure the braking distance of its cars on different surfaces.

Which of the following surfaces is likely to have the shortest braking distance?

Draw a circle around the correct answer.

wet road   **icy road**   **dry road**

[1 mark]

b The car manufacturer tests their car again after it has driven 65,000 miles. It has had new tyres, but the brake pads are old.

What is the likely to happen to the braking distance?

Draw a circle around the correct answer.

decreases   **increases**   **stays the same**

[1 mark]

2. **a** Use the correct answers from the box below to complete the sentences.

braking distance   **thinking distance**

Being drunk is likely to increase a driver's _____ .

Driving with four new tyres is likely to decrease the _____ of
a car.   [2 marks]

b Complete the sentence.

The distance the car travels from when the driver sees an event to when

the car comes to a complete stop is called the _____ .   [1 mark]

3. Hamza is driving a racing car.

Why does it have a shorter braking distance than an ordinary car?

Tick **two** boxes.

☐ It has a higher top speed.

☐ Its brakes are bigger and stronger.

☐ The tyres are wider, resulting in better grip.

☐ Hamza's reaction times are faster.

☐ Hamza presses the brake pedal harder. [2 marks]

4. The UK legal minimum limit for the depth of tyre treads is 1.6 millimetres.

Old tyres

New tyres

How would you explain to someone why their tyres would be dangerous in wet weather if they are worn down?

_____

_____

_____

_____ [2 marks]

Outcome 10: Atoms and nuclear radiation

- Some atoms have an unstable nucleus. When a nucleus randomly decays it emits (gives off) ionising radiation.
- Nuclear radiation can be an alpha particle, a beta particle or a gamma ray.
- Gamma rays are the most penetrating radiation and have the longest range.
- Alpha particles are the least penetrating source and have the shortest range.
- Ionising radiation can be dangerous if handled carelessly, because it can damage living cells. But it can also be useful.

1. Use the correct answer from the box to label the diagram of an atom.

alpha particle	atom	beta particle	nucleus

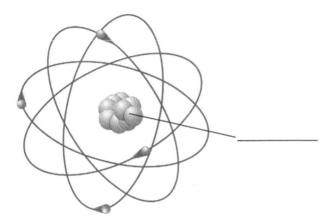

[1 mark]

2. Different types of nuclear radiation get stopped by different materials.

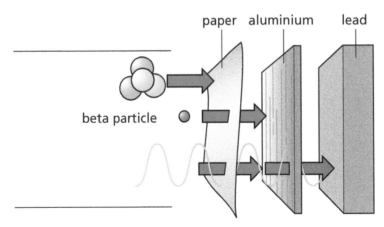

Use the correct answers from the box to label the diagram.

alpha particle	gamma ray	nucleus	atom

[2 marks]

3. Alpha particles have a shorter range than gamma rays and beta particles.

Why does this make alpha sources less dangerous if you walk near them?

_____

_____ [1 mark]

4. The column on the left lists different types of radiation.

The column on the right lists some uses of radiation.

Draw **one** line from each type of radiation to an example of how it can be used.

Type		Use
Alpha particles		measuring the thickness of aluminium foil
Beta particles		sterilising medical equipment
Gamma rays		smoke detectors

[3 marks]

5. Three radioactive sources are placed inside boxes made of different materials.

GCSE Grade 1

A radioactivity sensor is used to see if the radiation is leaving each container.

Will the radioactivity be detected for each source?

Tick **three** boxes.

	Detected	Not detected
Alpha source in thick lead box — Detector		
Beta source in paper bag — Detector		
Gamma source in aluminium foil — Detector		

[3 marks]

Mini test

1. A funicular railway is stopped at the bottom of a hill (A). It is then pulled up a hill until it comes to a stop again at the top (B).

Use the correct answers from the boxes to complete the sentences. [2 marks]
Outcome 1

| less | more | the same |

At B the train has _____ gravitational potential energy than at A.

At B the train has _____ kinetic energy as at A.

2. Why does insulating your loft reduce the cost of heating your house? [1 mark]
Outcome 2

_____

_____

3. Which of the following power stations are powered by fossil fuels? [2 marks]
Outcome 3

Tick **two** boxes.

☐ coal power stations

☐ hydroelectric power stations

☐ oil power stations

☐ tidal power stations

☐ nuclear power stations

4. Which of the following are contact forces? [3 marks]

Outcome 4

Tick **three** boxes.

☐ air resistance

☐ friction

☐ magnetic

☐ gravitational

☐ tension (in a string)

5. Meesha is emptying her garage. She finds it difficult to push heavy boxes around.

She puts the boxes on a trolley with wheels. This is much easier for her to push over the same distance.

Use the correct answers from the boxes to complete the sentences. You may use the answers more than once. [3 marks]

Outcome 5

| friction | goes down | goes up | mass | stays the same | weight |

By putting the box on the trolley, the force required to move it

_____.

By putting the box on the trolley, the total work done pushing it

_____.

The reason it is easier to push the box on the trolley is because there is less

_____.

6. Terry cycles 60 kilometres.

It takes him 2 hours.

What was Terry's average speed? [1 mark]
Outcome 6

_____

_____

Average speed = _____ kilometres per hour.

7. The column on the left lists some phrases used to describe braking.

The column on the right lists some descriptions.

Draw **one** line from each word to its definition. [3 marks]
Outcome 7

Phrase	Description

Braking distance

the distance the car travels during the driver's reaction time

Stopping distance

the distance the car travels once the brakes have been pressed

Thinking distance

the distance a car travels from when the driver sees an event to when it comes to a stop

8. Quinn and Romeo do an experiment to test Romeo's reaction times.

a What is the best way to do the experiment? [1 mark]
Outcome 8

Tick **one** box.

☐ Quinn drops and catches the ruler while Romeo times it with a stop watch.

☐ Romeo drops and catches the ruler while Quinn records the distance it fell.

☐ Quinn drops the ruler and Romeo catches it as quickly as he can, and they record the distance it fell.

b Which of the following statements is true?   [1 mark]
                                                                    Outcome 8

Tick **one** box.

☐ The further the ruler travels the slower the reaction time.

☐ The further the ruler travels the faster the reaction time.

9. Trains cannot stop quickly or swerve to avoid accidents.

A train with seven carriages is travelling at 100 kilometres per hour. The braking distance is tested.

It is tested in the following conditions.

Track conditions	Braking distance (km)
Dry track	1.1
Wet track	1.3
Leaves on the track	1.4

a What type of track conditions has the longest braking distance?

Draw a circle around the correct answer.   [1 mark]
                                                                  Outcome 9

dry track   **wet track**   **leaves on the track**

b Why is the total stopping distance longer than the braking distance measured?   [1 mark]
                                                                  Outcome 7

_____

_____

10. Which type of radiation can penetrate through 1 cm of aluminium?   [1 mark]
                                                                  Outcome 10
Draw a circle around the correct answer.

alpha particles   **beta particles**   **gamma rays**

Total: 20 marks

Outcome 1: Electric current

- Electric current is a flow of electric charges.
- The size of the electric current is the rate of flow of electric charge.
- Electric current through a component depends on its resistance and the voltage across it.
- The resistance of a component is a measure of how difficult it is for an electric current to pass through it.
- If voltage is kept the same, when resistance goes up, current will go down.

1. Describe an electric current by completing the sentence using the correct answer from the box.

Tip
An electrical component is one part of a whole circuit, such as a battery or a resistor.

voltage	current	charge

The flow of electric _____ is called an electric current.   [1 mark]

2. Metals are good conductors.

The diagram shows how metals contain electric charges.

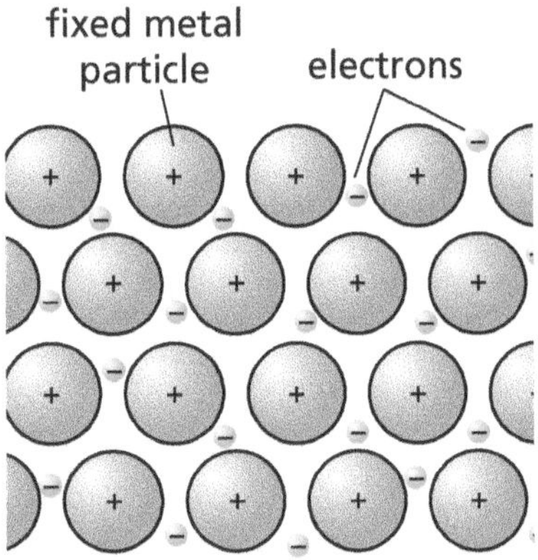

What is the name for the electric charges that flow as a current when the metal is connected in a circuit?

fixed metal particle   electrons

Tick **one** box.

☐ current   ☐ electrons   ☐ metal   ☐ resistance   [1 mark]

3. Complete the sentences to describe the steps to investigate electrical conductors.

Use the correct answers from the box.

battery	charge	circuit	conductor	voltage

Select a _____, wires, a lamp and materials for testing.

Connect the battery, lamp and material in a complete _____.

If the lamp lights, then the material is a _____ because it has allowed the current to flow.   [3 marks]

4. Special words are used when describing electricity.

The column on the left lists some key words.

The column on the right lists some definitions.

Draw **one** line from each term to its correct definition.

Keywords

Definition

| a measure of how difficult it is for an electric current to pass through a component |

Resistance

| the flow of electrical charge |

Current

| the push of electrons through an electric circuit |

[2 marks]

5. Rajnee builds an electric circuit to take some measurements.

GCSE Grade 1

The diagram below shows the circuit.

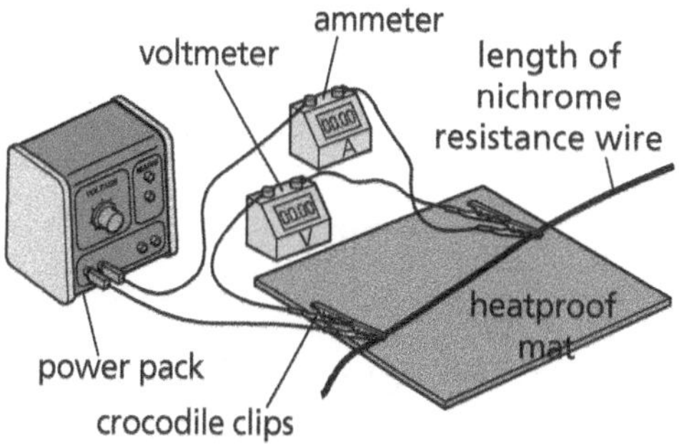

a Name the part of the circuit that is used to measure current.

Draw a circle around the correct answer.

ammeter **thermometer** **voltmeter** [1 mark]

b Name the part of the circuit that is used to measure voltage.

Draw a circle around the correct answer.

ammeter **thermometer** **voltmeter** [1 mark]

c If the circuit voltage is kept the same, what happens to the current if the resistance is made larger?

Choose the correct answer from the box to complete the sentence.

larger **smaller** **stay the same**

If resistance is made larger, current will become _____. [1 mark]

Outcome 2: a.c. and d.c. current

- A complete circuit is necessary for a current to flow.
- A battery is two or more cells joined in a circuit.
- Cells and batteries supply current that always passes in the same direction. This is called direct current (d.c.).
- An alternating current (a.c.) is one that changes direction.
- Mains electricity is an a.c. supply.
- In the UK, mains electricity has a frequency of 50 hertz and voltage of 230 volts.

1. The picture shows a simple circuit that includes a battery.

What type of current is produced when cells and batteries are the energy source for an electric circuit? [1 mark]

Tick **one** box.

☐ alternating current

☐ direct current

☐ domestic current

☐ mains current

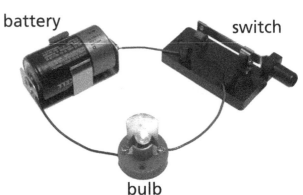
battery   switch
bulb

2. The column on the left lists keywords used to describe mains electricity.

The column on the right lists some statements about mains electricity in the UK.

Draw **one** line from each word to the statement that describes it.

Keyword	Statement
Alternating current (a.c.)	alternating current is delivered to UK houses at 230 volts
Frequency	current that changes direction
Voltage	alternating current changes direction and back again at 50 hertz (50 times per second) in the UK

[3 marks]

3. **a** How does direct current move?

Draw a circle around the correct answer.

d.c. changes direction   **d.c. moves in the same direction**

it depends on the circuit   [1 mark]

b How does alternating current move?

Draw a circle around the correct answer.

a.c. changes direction   **a.c. moves in the same direction**

it depends on the circuit   [1 mark]

4. The diagram show two lamps connected to a battery by wires.

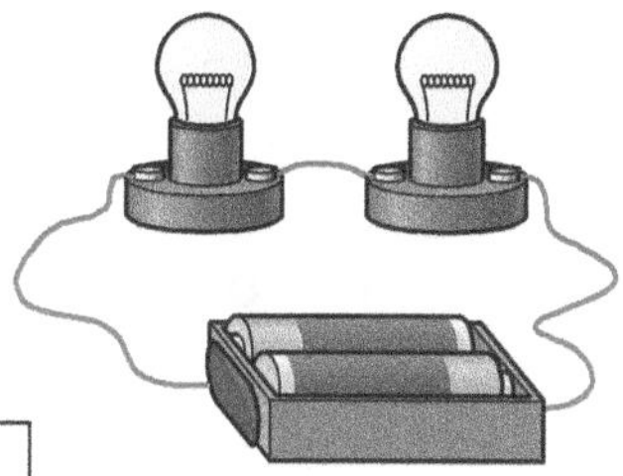

Use the correct answers from the box to complete the sentences.

battery	**complete**	**direct**	**gaps**

A current will flow because this is a _____ circuit.

This means there are no _____ between the components.

The cells in the battery supply _____ current.   [3 marks]

5. In buildings in the UK, the mains electricity is arranged using a system of loops of wires called a ring main.

GCSE Grade 1

The diagram shows the ring main supplies to plug sockets.

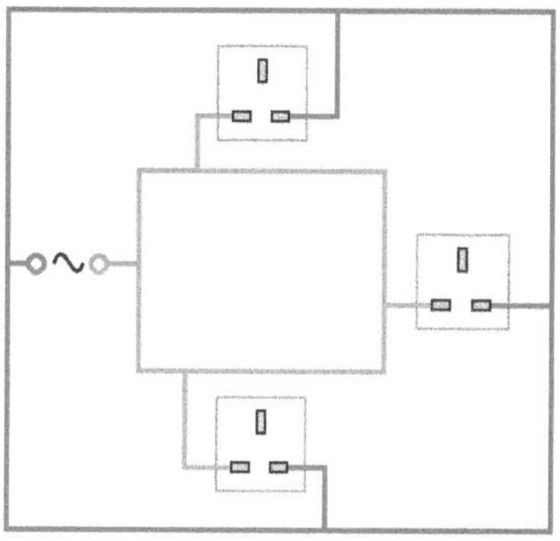

Which statements about a ring main are true?

Tick **two** boxes.

☐ The ring main carries a direct current.

☐ The ring main has a voltage of 230 V.

☐ The ring main is an alternating current.

☐ The ring main has a frequency of 100 Hz.

Tip

Remember that mains electricity is the electricity supplied to buildings from power stations.

☐ The ring main always passes current in the same direction.   [2 marks]

Outcome 3: Electrical appliances and safety

- Most electrical appliances are connected to the mains using three-core flex.
- The insulation covering each wire in the flex is colour-coded for easy identification:
  - o live wire – brown
  - o neutral wire – blue
  - o earth wire – green and yellow stripes.
- The earth wire is a safety wire. It stops the appliance becoming live.
- The fuse contains a thin piece of wire, which melts if the current becomes too large. This cuts the power supply off.
- Some appliances do not have an earth wire because they are double insulated.

1. The picture shows the type of wire that is used to connect most electrical appliances to the mains plug. What is the name for this wire?

   Tick **one** box.

   ☐ earth wire   ☐ thin fuse wire

   ☐ three-core flex   ☐ insulation   [1 mark]

2. The diagram shows the wires inside a three-pin plug.

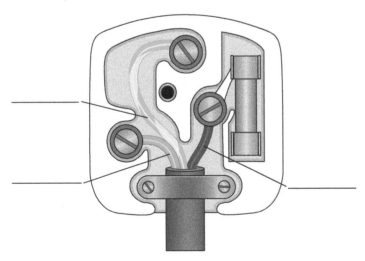

   Use the correct answers from the box to label the diagram.   [3 marks]

neutral wire   live wire   earth wire

3. Electrical appliances need to be handled with care and safety features are important. Fuses are used in plugs as a safety feature.

a Name the wire in a plug that is connected to the fuse.

_____ [1 mark]

b Rearrange the sentences to explain how the fuse in a plug works.

A. The circuit is broken and the electricity supply is cut off.

B. The current in an appliance becomes too large.

C. The thin wire in the fuse gets very hot and melts.

Write the letters in the correct order in the boxes below.

[2 marks]

4. Some appliances, such as hairdryers, are double insulated so they do not need an earth wire.

GCSE Grade 1

Use the correct answers from the box to complete each sentence. [3 marks]

| casing | earth | metal | plastic | wire |

Appliances that are double insulated have an inner casing made from an

electrical insulator, such as _____.

This prevents the live _____ from touching the outer

_____ if it becomes loose.

Double insulation is a safety feature and protects the user from electrical shock.

Outcome 4: Electrical appliances and energy transfer

- Electrical appliances transfer energy.
- The amount of energy transferred depends on the power and how long the appliance is switched on.
- Power is the rate of energy transfer.
- Energy (kilowatt-hours or kWh) = power (kilowatts or kW) × time (hours).

1. Electrical appliances are used to transfer energy.

   The energy transferred depends on how long the appliance is switched on for and one other factor.

   What is the other factor?

   Tick **one** box.

   ☐ The power of the appliance.

   ☐ The colour of the appliance.

   ☐ If the appliance is new.

   ☐ If the appliance has been safety tested. [1 mark]

2. Each of these appliances has been labelled with its power rating in watts (W).

   Microwave oven: 1000 W   Toaster: 1200 W   Laptop computer: 20 W

   Work out the power ratings as kilowatts (kW).

   Tip
   Remember to divide by 1000 when converting watts to kilowatts.

   microwave oven: 1000 watts = _____ kilowatts

   toaster: 1200 watts = _____ kilowatts

   laptop computer: 20 watts = _____ kilowatts [3 marks]

3. The energy transferred by an electrical appliance is calculated using the equation

energy transferred = power × time

Choose the correct answer from the box to complete the sentence.

hours	minutes	seconds

To calculate the energy transferred in kWh by an electrical appliance,

the correct unit of time to use is _____.   [1 mark]

4. Use the equation in the box to calculate the amount of energy (in kilowatt-hours) transferred by an electric oven with a power of 2150 watts that is switched on for 30 minutes.

GCSE Grade 1

energy = power × time

_____

_____

_____

Energy transferred = _____ kWh   [3 marks]

Outcome 5: Magnets and magnetic fields

- The poles of a magnet are the places where the magnetic forces are strongest.
- When two magnets are brought close together they exert a force on each other.
- Attraction is a pulling force. Repulsion is a pushing force.
- Two like poles repel each other. Two unlike poles attract each other.
- Attraction and repulsion between two magnetic poles are examples of non-contact forces.

1. Marcus investigates how magnets can exert (make happen) forces on other magnets.

   Choose one type of observation that he sees when moving magnets close together.

   Tick **one** box.

   ☐ Like poles attract each other.

   ☐ Like poles repel each other.

   ☐ Unlike poles repel each other. [1 mark]

2. Complete the diagram of the second magnet to show which pole of your magnet would be attracted to the S pole of the magnet shown. [1 mark]

   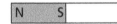

3. a The diagram shows the magnetic force between two unlike poles.

   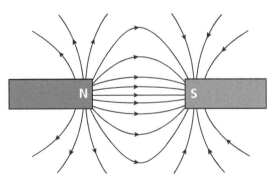

   Use the correct answers from the box to complete the sentences.

attracting	pulling	pushing	repelling

Unlike poles interact by _____ each other.

The force between two unlike poles is a _____ force. [2 marks]

b The diagram shows the magnetic force between two like poles.

Complete the sentences below using words from the box.

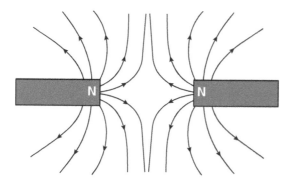

Use the correct answers from the box to complete the sentences.

attracting   pulling   pushing   repelling

Like poles interact by _____ each other.

The force from one north pole on another north pole is a

_____ force. [2 marks]

4. Sam and Alex investigate how magnets can attract and repel each other. They push and pull magnets along a surface without the magnets touching.

Name the term to describe this type of force.

_____ [1 mark]

5. Draw the magnetic field pattern around a bar magnet.

GCSE Grade 1

[3 marks]

N   S

Outcome 6: Electromagnets

- When a current flows through a conducting wire a magnetic field is produced around the wire.
- The strength of the magnetic field depends on
  o the current through the wire
  o the distance from the wire.
- The magnetic field strength around a current-carrying wire can be increased by
  o shaping a wire into a coil called a solenoid
  o adding an iron core
  o increasing the current.

1. The diagram shows a current flowing through a conducting wire and the magnetic field produced.

   The strength of the magnetic field changes as the distance from the wire increases.

   Use the correct answers from the box to complete the sentence.

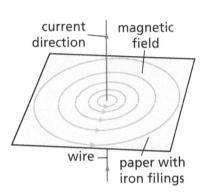

decreases	stays the same	increases

   As distance from the wire _____, the

   strength of the magnetic field _____.

   Tip
   Look at the magnetic field lines to help you.

   [2 marks]

2. The diagram shows one way of making the magnetic field of a solenoid stronger.

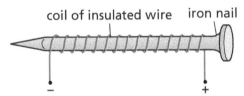

   a Explain how the solenoid in the diagram has been made stronger.

   _____

   _____ [1 mark]

b Suggest another way of making the magnetic field in a solenoid stronger.

_____

_____ [1 mark]

3. Electromagnets have many uses.

Choose the correct answers from the box to complete each sentence.

current	magnetism	stronger	weaker

An electromagnet is useful because it can be turned off by switching off the

_____. This means the magnetic field can be controlled.

Iron is used in the electromagnet to make it _____.

Iron loses its _____ when the current is switched off. [3 marks]

4. Electromagnets are used in many ways. The photograph shows one way that electromagnets can be used in a scrapyard.

GCSE Grade 1

Explain why using the electromagnet in the picture works better than using an ordinary magnet.

_____

_____

_____

_____ [2 marks]

Outcome 7: Transverse and longitudinal waves

- Waves may be either transverse or longitudinal.
- In a transverse wave the direction of energy transfer is at a right-angle to the movement of the wave. Ripples moving up and down on the surface of water and light are example of transverse waves.
- In a longitudinal wave the direction of energy transfer is in the same direction as the movement of the wave. Sound waves travelling through air are longitudinal waves.
- Longitudinal waves show areas of compression (squashed together) and rarefaction (stretched out).

1. The picture shows a slinky being used to model transverse and longitudinal waves.

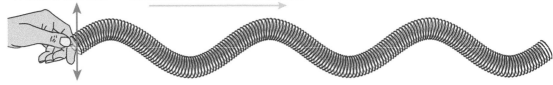

Transverse wave   direction of wave movement

Longitudinal wave

direction of wave movement

   a Choose the correct term to describe a visible light wave.

Draw a circle around the correct answer.

longitudinal   **ripple**   **transverse**   **vacuum**   [1 mark]

   b Choose the correct term to describe a sound wave.

Draw a circle around the correct answer.

longitudinal   **ripple**   **transverse**   **vacuum**   [1 mark]

2. Oscillate means moving from one point to another and back in a regular cycle.

The column on the left lists the two types of waves.

The column on the right lists descriptions of them.

Draw **one** line from each type of wave to the description of how it oscillates during the transfer of energy.

Type of wave	Description

oscillations are parallel to the direction of energy transfer

Transverse wave

oscillations only occur in a vacuum

Longitudinal wave

oscillations are perpendicular (at right-angles) to the direction of energy transfer

oscillations only occur in water

[2 marks]

3. The speaker in the diagram is producing sound waves in air.

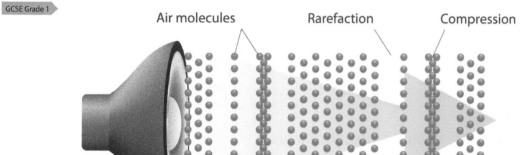

Air molecules   Rarefaction   Compression

Use the correct answers from the box to complete each sentence.

You may use the answers more than once.

particles	closer together	further apart

Compression is the part of the longitudinal wave where _____ are

_____ than when the wave is not present.

Rarefaction is the part of the longitudinal wave where _____ are

_____ than when the wave is not present.   [4 marks]

Outcome 8: Wave characteristics

- Waves are described by their amplitude, wavelength and frequency.
- The amplitude of a wave is the highest or lowest point on a wave away from its undisturbed position.
- The wavelength of a wave is the distance from a point on one wave to the same point on the next wave.
- The frequency of a wave is the number of waves passing a point each second.
- You can calculate the speed of a wave speed from its frequency and wavelength:

  wave speed = frequency × wavelength
- Frequency is measured in units called hertz (Hz).

1. The diagrams below show different waves.

Which wave shows exactly two wavelengths?

Tick **one** box.

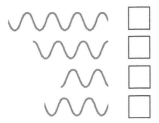

[1 mark]

2. Use the correct answers to label the diagram.

Use each word twice.

amplitude	wavelength

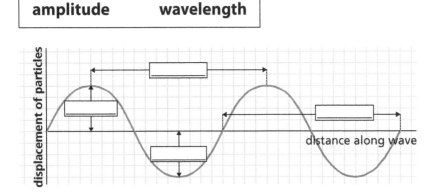

[2 marks]

3. Graphs are used to analyse waves.

What is the word use to describe the maximum displacement of a point on a wave?

Draw a circle around the correct answer.

amplitude   frequency   wavelength   [1 mark]

4. The graphs show different waves.

Wave A   Wave B   Wave C   Wave D

a Which wave has the longest wavelength?

Draw a circle around the correct answer.

Wave A   Wave B   Wave C   Wave D   [1 mark]

b The diagrams above show each wave for one second.

Find the frequency for Wave A and Wave B.

Wave A: _____ hertz.

Wave B: _____ hertz   [2 marks]

5. A wave has a frequency of 1650 hertz and a wavelength of 20 centimetres.

a Convert the wavelength from centimetres to metres.

20 centimetres = _____ metres   [1 mark]

b Use this equation to calculate the speed of the wave.

wave speed = frequency × wavelength

Wave speed = _____

_____

Wave speed = _____ metres per second   [2 marks]

Outcome 9: Electromagnetic waves

- Electromagnetic waves are transverse waves.
- Electromagnetic waves form a continuous spectrum.
- Electromagnetic waves are grouped by their wavelength and frequency: radio, microwave, infrared, visible light (red to violet), ultraviolet, X-rays, gamma rays.
- All electromagnetic waves travel at the same speed. This is the same in a vacuum and air.
- Ultraviolet waves, X-rays and gamma rays can damage human body tissue. The effects depend on the type of radiation and the size of the dose.

Use this diagram of the electromagnetic spectrum to help you answer the questions.

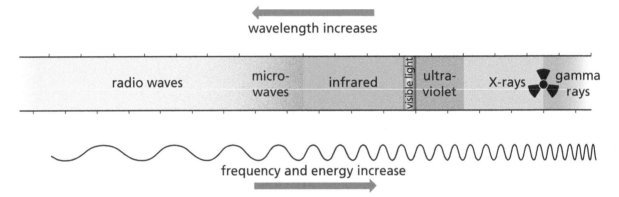

1. The column on the left lists some types of electromagnet waves.

   The column on the right lists the position of these waves in the electromagnetic spectrum.

   Draw **one** line from each type of wave to its position in the spectrum.

Type of wave	Position
Ultraviolet waves	between radio waves and infrared waves
X-rays	between visible light waves and X-rays
Microwaves	between ultraviolet waves and gamma rays

[3 marks]

2. **a** Which part of the electromagnetic spectrum has a lower frequency than visible light waves?

Tick **one** box.

☐ gamma rays ☐ ultraviolet waves

☐ X-rays ☐ infrared waves [1 mark]

b Name one part of the electromagnetic spectrum that carries less energy than visible light.

_____ [1 mark]

3. Answer these questions.

What are the highest frequency waves? _____

Which waves have the longest wavelength? _____

Which waves carry less energy than gamma waves but more than

ultraviolet waves? _____ [3 marks]

4. **a** Identify two types of electromagnetic waves that have high frequency and are hazardous to human body cells.

Draw **two** circles, one around each correct answer.

radio waves **gamma rays** **visible light** **X-rays** [2 marks]

b Describe two ways we can reduce the harmful effects of the waves identified in part **a**.

_____

_____

_____

_____ [2 marks]

Outcome 10: Uses of electromagnetic waves

- Electromagnetic waves have many practical applications from speed cameras to space telescopes.
- Other uses include
    - radio waves – television and radio (including Bluetooth) and radar
    - microwaves – satellite communications, cooking food
    - infrared – electrical heaters, cooking food, infrared (thermal) cameras
    - visible light – lighting, fibre optic communications
    - ultraviolet – energy efficient lamps, sun tanning
    - X-rays – medical imaging and treatments
    - gamma rays – sterilising.

Use the diagram of the electromagnetic spectrum on page 146 to help you answer the questions.

1. The Sun gives out a lot of visible light.

    We see the world around us using this part of the electromagnetic spectrum.

    Name one more use of visible light.

    Tick **one** box.

    ☐ fibre-optic communications   ☐ satellite communications

    ☐ sterilising medical equipment   ☐ tanning sun beds   [1 mark]

2. Electromagnetic waves have many uses.

    The column on the left lists some electromagnetic waves.

    The column on the right lists some uses.

    Draw one line from each type of electromagnetic wave to one of its uses.

Electromagnetic waves	**Uses**
Infrared waves	cooking food
Microwaves	desk lamp
Light waves	heating

    [3 marks]

3. The table shows uses of high energy waves in the electromagnetic spectrum.

Complete the table by adding the type of wave used in each application.

Use	Type of wave
Sterilising medical equipment and treating cancer	
Sun tanning and security marking lamp	
Medical imaging for diagnosis and treatments	

[3 marks]

4. Ania uses a remote control to switch on the TV.

Normally no light is seen from the remote control.

When the remote control is viewed through a digital camera, a light from the remote control can be seen, as shown in the photograph.

a Name the waves that are being emitted from the TV remote control.

_____ [1 mark]

b Complete the sentence to explain why a light is seen on the remote control through the digital camera, but cannot normally be seen.

The digital camera detects _____ waves but

our _____ cannot. [2 marks]

Mini test

1. The diagram shows an electrical circuit with two lamps and two cells.

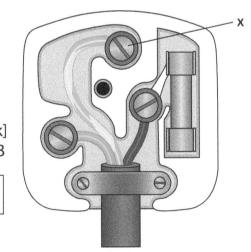

  a An ammeter can be added to this circuit. What will the ammeter measure?

  Draw a circle around the correct answer.

  [1 mark]
  Outcome 1

  current   **resistance**   **voltage**

  b What is the correct name for cells connected like this?

  Tick **one** box.

  [1 mark]
  Outcome 2

  ☐ battery   ☐ charger   ☐ double cell

2. What is the voltage of the mains electricity supply in the UK?

Draw a circle around the correct answer.

[1 mark]
Outcome 2

  12 joules   **13 hertz**   **50 amps**   **230 volts**

3. The diagram shows the inside of a three-pin plug.

  a Which wire is connected to pin X?

  Choose the correct answer from the box.   [1 mark]
  Outcome 3

  | earth wire   live wire   neutral wire |

  _____

b What is the purpose of the live wire? [1 mark]
Outcome 3

_____

c Which component will melt and break the circuit if the current is too high? [1 mark]
Outcome 3

_____

4. **a** Choose the correct power rating of the kettle in kilowatts (kW). [1 mark]
Outcome 4

electric kettle, 2000 W    toaster, 1.2 kW

Tick **one** box.

☐ 0.2 kW ☐ 2 kW

☐ 20 kW ☐ 200 kW

b Use the equation to work out how much energy is transferred by the toaster in 3 minutes (0.05 hours). [1 mark]
Outcome 4

Energy (kWh) = power (kW) × time (h)

_____

_____

The toaster transfers _____ kilowatt-hours of energy.

5. The diagram shows the magnetic field between two bar magnets.

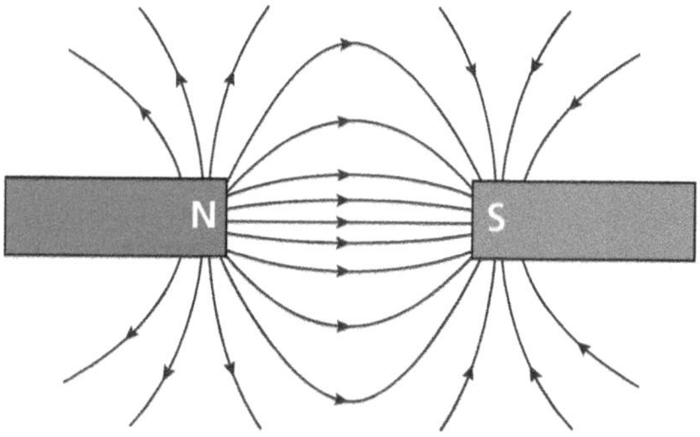

Describe the force between the poles of the two magnets. [1 mark]
Outcome 5

N | S

Tick **one** box.

☐ They strongly attract. ☐ There is no force. ☐ They strongly repel.

6. The diagram below shows an electromagnet as part of a doorbell circuit.

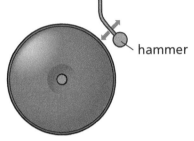

a Identify the part labelled X.

[1 mark]

Outcome 6

_____

b Why is an iron core used and not a permanent magnet? [1 mark]

Outcome 6

_____

_____

7. **a** What type of wave is shown in the diagram?

Choose the correct answer from the box. [1 mark]

Outcome 7

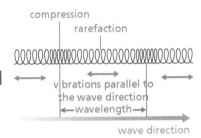

| longitudinal wave | transverse wave | water wave |

_____

b What type of wave is shown in the diagram below?

Choose the correct answer from the box.

| longitudinal wave | sound wave |
| transverse wave |

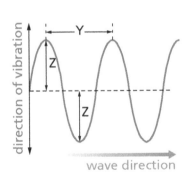

[1 mark]

Outcome 7

_____

c What is identified by the letter Y in the diagram above? [1 mark]

Outcome 8

_____

d What is identified by the letter Z in the diagram above? [1 mark]
Outcome 8

_____

8. The diagram shows the electromagnetic spectrum in order of decreasing wavelength.

Two types of wave are missing from the diagram.

decreasing wavelength →

radio waves		infrared waves	visible light waves		X-rays	gamma rays

a What is the missing type of wave that has a longer wavelength than infrared waves? [1 mark]
Outcome 9

_____

b What is the missing type of wave that has higher frequency than visible light waves? [1 mark]
Outcome 9

_____

9. The column on the left lists regions of the electromagnetic spectrum.

The column on the right lists uses of the electromagnetic spectrum.

Draw **one** line from each region of the electromagnetic spectrum to their correct use.

We have done one to help you.

Region	Use
Infrared waves	medical imaging of bones
Visible light waves	cooking food
X-rays	**sun tanning beds**
Ultraviolet waves	fibre-optic communications

[3 marks]
Outcome 10

Total: 20 marks

Progress tracker

Tick off each outcome when you have completed the questions and feel confident about this topic.

Component	Outcomes				
Component 1 – Biology: The human body	1: Cells ✓	2: Tissues, organs and systems ✓	3: The digestive system ✓	4: Respiration and lifestyle ✓	5: Pathogens ✓
Component 2 – Biology: Environment, evolution and inheritance	1: Feeding relationships ✓	2: Adaptation ✓	3: Food chains and webs ✓	4: Recycling materials ✓	5: Competition ✓
Component 3 – Chemistry: Elements, mixtures and compounds	1: Atoms and elements ✓	2: Making compounds ✓	3: States of matter ✓	4: Diamond and graphite ✓	5: Separating mixtures ✓
Component 4 – Chemistry: Chemistry in our world	1: Acids and salts ✓	2: Neutralisation ✓	3: Energy transfers in chemistry ✓	4: Rate of reaction ✓	5: The early atmosphere ✓
Component 5 – Physics: Energy, forces and the structure of matter	1: Energy changes ✓	2: Energy transfers ✓	3: Energy resources ✓	4: Contact and non-contact forces ✓	5: Work ✓
Component 6 – Physics: Electricity, magnetism and waves	1: Electric current ✓	2: a.c. and d.c. current ✓	3: Electrical appliances and safety ✓	4: Electrical appliances and energy transfer ✓	5: Magnets and magnetic fields ✓

Outcomes				
6: Fighting disease ✓	7: Drugs ✓	8: Control systems ✓	9: Hormones ✓	10: Controlling fertility ✓
6: Abiotic and biotic factors ✓	7: Pollution ✓	8: Evolution ✓	9: Reproduction ✓	10: DNA, genes and chromosomes ✓
6: Paper chromatography ✓	7: Extracting metals ✓	8: Metals ✓	9: Alloys ✓	10: Polymers ✓
6: The atmosphere today ✓	7: Crude oil ✓	8: Burning fuels ✓	9: Greenhouse gases ✓	10: Water for drinking ✓
6: Speed ✓	7: Stopping distances ✓	8: Reaction times ✓	9: Braking distance ✓	10: Atoms and nuclear radiation ✓
6: Electromagnets ✓	7: Transverse and longitudinal waves ✓	8: Wave characteristics ✓	9: Electromagnetic waves ✓	10: Uses of electromagnetic waves ✓

Biology

Abiotic: Non-living factor of an ecosystem.

Absorbed: Or 'taken in'; useful products from digestion are absorbed through the wall of the intestine into the blood.

Acid rain: When sulfur dioxide and other gases such as oxides of nitrogen dissolve in rain water an acidic solution known as 'acid rain' is formed.

Action: Any response which our body carries out, such as kicking, walking or blinking.

Adapted: An adapted organism has characteristics to suit the conditions where it lives. For example, a polar bear has thick, white fur.

Addictive: An addictive substance is one that your body becomes dependent on: once you start taking it, you want more and it is difficult to give up.

Algae: Organisms previously thought of as plants. Algae have chlorophyll but lack true stems, roots, and leaves.

Antibiotic: A drug that acts on bacteria.

Antibody: A substance produced by the body to fight disease. Antibodies are proteins that are produced by the immune system.

Asexual reproduction: A way of reproducing new identical offspring from only one parent.

Automatic: A response happens without thinking about it; we cannot control automatic reactions.

Bacteria: Simple microscopic single-celled organisms; some are good for the body, others can cause illness and disease.

Biotic: Living components that affect population size or the environment such as predators.

Blood: A fluid that our heart pumps around our whole body.

Brain: A large organ inside the skull; it receives and processes information from body sensors and uses this information to make decisions.

Carbon cycle: How carbon is recycled so that it can be used again.

Carbon dioxide: a gas produced by burning fossil fuels and by respiration.

Cell: The unit of a living organism that contains the parts to carry out life processes.

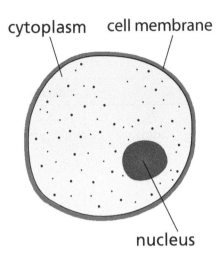

cytoplasm   cell membrane

nucleus

Cell Membrane: Surrounds the cell and controls movement of substances in and out.

Characteristics: The features that distinguish one person from another, for example the shape of nose or colour of eyes.

Chlorophyll: The green pigment in plants and algae, which absorbs light energy.

Chromosomes: The thread-like structures containing tightly coiled DNA.

Clone: An organism that is genetically identical to another organism.

Competition: When two or more living things struggle against each other to get the same resource.

Consumer: Feeds on another organism.

Contraceptive: A method designed to prevent the fertilisation of an egg.

Coordinated: If processes are coordinated it means that they are working together for the same purpose.

Cutting: A piece of a plant (often a leaf) that is cut off; it can then be planted in soil to grow a new plant.

Cytoplasm: A jelly-like substance where most chemical processes happen.

Decay: How living things are broken down when the die.

Deforestation: The cutting down and removal of forests.

Digestion: The process of breaking down food into simple substances that can be absorbed into the blood.

DNA: The material found in the nucleus of cells that contains genetic information.

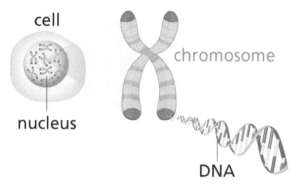

cell

nucleus

chromosome

DNA

Drug: A substance not normally found in the body that is taken to bring about a particular effect.

Ecosystem: The living things in a given area and its habitat.

Egg: The female reproductive cell; when fertilised it can develop into an embryo.

Environment: The surrounding where an organism lives.

Enzymes: Substances that speed up the chemical reactions of digestion.

Evolution: Theory that the animal and plant species living today descended from species that existed in the past.

Extinct: When no more individuals of a species remain.

Fertility: The natural ability to produce another living being; if a woman is fertile it means that she can produce a baby.

Food chain: Shows what eats what in a habitat; it shows the flow of energy from one organism to the next, starting with a producer, ending with a top predator.

Food web: Shows how food chains in an ecosystem are linked.

Fossils: The preserved remains or traces of animals, plants and other organisms from the past.

Gall bladder: A storage organ that helps in the digestion of fat by storing bile.

Gene: A section of DNA that determines an inherited characteristic; genes are held on the chromosome.

Genetic: Genetic material controls inherited characteristics such as eye colour.

Genetic engineering: Transplanting genes for a desired characteristic into a different organism.

Glands: Organs in the body that make hormones.

Gullet: A tube connecting the mouth to the stomach.

Habitat: A place where something lives.

Heart: A large organ in the chest that pumps blood around the body.

Herbicide: A weed killer, used to kill unwanted plants.

Hormone: A chemical messenger that carries a signal from one cell (or group of cells) to another via the blood.

Ingest: Consume.

Inhibit: To prevent.

Kidneys: A pair of organs in the body that are responsible for removing some of the liquid waste products.

Landfill sites: These are sites where waste material can be buried in the ground; they are often used to dispose of household rubbish.

Large intestine: Lower part of the intestine where water is absorbed and where faeces are formed.

Liver: A large organ. It does many things, including cleaning the blood of toxins.

Mature: To grow to full size.

Menstrual cycle: This is a recurring series of changes that occur in a woman's body; these changes are brought about by hormones and are linked to reproduction.

Microorganism: An organism that is too small to be seen with the naked eye but can be seen under a microscope. Microorganisms include bacteria, viruses and some fungi. Many of these microorganisms are very useful to us because they break down waste products.

Nucleus: Contains genetic material (DNA), which controls the cell's activities.

Nutrients: Are substances that all living things need in order to survive; plants get their nutrients from the soil; animals get their nutrients from eating plants or other animals.

Offspring: The young animals or plants that are produced by the parent(s) as a result of reproduction.

Oral: Taken into the body through the mouth.

Organ: Group of different tissues working together to carry out a job.

Organism: A living animal, plant or microorganism.

Oxygen: A gas found in the air that we use in respiration.

Pancreas: A large gland behind the stomach; it releases digestive enzymes into the small intestine and releases hormones into the bloodstream.

Pathogen: A microorganism that causes disease.

Penicillin: A type of antibiotic; it was one of the first ones to be produced.

Pesticide: A toxic substance used to kill living things such as insects.

Photosynthesis: A process where plants and algae turn carbon dioxide and water into glucose (food) and releases oxygen.

Plants: Living things that can produce their own food by photosynthesis.

Plasmid: The small circular genetic material present in bacterial cells and used in genetic engineering or genetic modification.

Pollution: Contamination that can harm living organisms.

Predator: An animal that hunts, kills and eats other animals.

Prey: An animal that is hunted and killed by another animal as food.

Producer: Green plant or algae that makes its own food using sunlight.

Pulse: A rhythmical throbbing that can be felt in an artery; it is caused by the heart pumping blood through the artery.

Pulse rate: The number of pulses that can be felt in a certain time.

Radiation: Transfer of energy as a wave.

Red blood cells: Carry oxygen around to all parts of the body.

Reflex action: A reflex is an automatic response of the body; it usually happens very rapidly and it often helps to protect our body.

Reproductive organs: Includes the testes in males and the ovaries in females.

Respiration: How living things use oxygen to release energy from food.

Saliva: A watery liquid produced in the mouth; it lubricates the food, making it easier to swallow, and starts the process of digestion.

Salivary glands: Produce saliva in your mouth.

Secreted: When hormones are released into the blood, they are said to be secreted.

Selective breeding: Breeding plants and animals for desirable genetic traits.

Sewage: Waste material such as urine and faeces that is taken away from homes through pipes and treated to make it harmless.

Sexual reproduction: A process by which a new individual animal or plant can be made; it involves two parents, one male and one female.

Small intestine: Upper part of the intestine where digestion is completed and nutrients are absorbed by the blood.

Stimulate: To provide a signal that will produce a response; eggs will not grow to maturity until they receive a signal to do so.

Stomach: A sac where food is mixed with acidic juices to start the digestion of protein and kill microorganisms.

Survival: The ability to stay alive.

Target organ: This is an organ in the body that receives the hormone and produces a response.

Territory: The area in which a plant or animal lives.

Theory: A well-supported explanation of some aspect of the natural world, based on a body of facts that have been repeatedly confirmed through observation and experiment.

Tissue: Group of cells of one type.

muscle tissue

Toxic: Poisonous.

Toxin: A type of poison.

Vaccination: Injection of a killed microbe in order to stimulate the immune system to protect us against the microbe, so preventing a disease.

Variety: Individual animals and plants that are not identical to each other, but which have slight differences.

Virus: The smallest type of microorganism; they can live inside body cells and cause disease.

White blood cell: One of the different types of cell found in the blood; they help us to fight diseases.

Chemistry

Acid: A substance that will turn litmus red, neutralise alkalis, and dissolve some metals.

Alkali: A soluble base. A substance that will turn litmus blue, neutralise acids, and dissolve some metals.

Alloy: A mixture of substances, at least one of which is a metal.

Aluminium: A silvery white metallic element not found in its natural state, but which has to be extracted from a compound in its ore.

Atmosphere: A layer of gases surrounding the surface of the Earth.

Atom: The smallest particle of an element that can exist.

Base: A solid substance that neutralises an acid: bases that dissolve in water are called alkalis.

Billion: A billion is a thousand million (1,000,000,000).

Biodegradable: A 'biodegradable' product breaks down, safely and relatively quickly, by biological means, into its raw materials.

Boiling point: The temperature at which a substance changes from a liquid to a gas.

Burning: Is sometimes called combustion; it is a chemical reaction in which a fuel combines with oxygen to release heat energy.

Carbon: Non-metallic element that can exist in different forms, such as soot, graphite or diamond.

Carbon dioxide: A gas produced by burning fossil fuels and by respiration; it turns limewater cloudy.

Carbon monoxide: A poisonous gas produced when fuels burn in a limited supply of oxygen.

Carbonate: A compound of carbon and oxygen that reacts with acids to release carbon dioxide.

Carbonates: Chemical compounds; they are formed when carbon dioxide reacts with an acid.

Catalyst: Substances that speed up chemical reactions but are unchanged at the end.

Chromatography: A process used to separate different soluble substances.

Combustion: Burning, in which a fuel combines with oxygen to release energy.

Compound: Two or more elements chemically joined together.

Conduct: Means 'to allow to pass through'. Metals let both electricity and heat flow through them easily.

Copper: A reddish-brown metallic element that is an excellent conductor of heat and electricity.

Corrosion: Air and water break the metal down.

Crude oil: A natural liquid product used as a raw material by oil refineries.

Crystallisation: A method of separating a solid that has dissolved in a liquid and made a solution. The excess water is evaporated and then the concentrated solution cools and crystals will start to grow.

Crystallised: A solid that was dissolved in a solution has formed crystals.

Distillation: A method to separate different liquids in a mixture which have different boiling points by boiling and condensing the liquids.

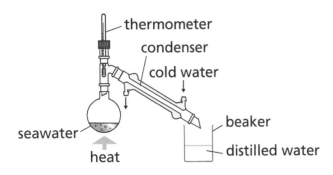

Elements: What all substances are made up of, and which contain only one type of atom.

Equation: A way of writing down what happens in a chemical reaction; instead of putting an 'equals' sign in the middle, an arrow pointing to the right is used.

Explosion: In the reaction, large amounts of gases are produced, and these expand very rapidly, blowing everything outward; explosions happen instantaneously.

Filtering: When water is filtered, it is strained through a sieve or mesh to remove solid particles; very small particles may be removed by filtering the water through sand.

Filtration: Separating an undissolved solid in a solution using a filter to produce a filtrate (liquid) and residue (solid).

Fossil fuels: Remains of dead organisms compacted over millions of years that are burned as fuels, releasing carbon dioxide.

Fraction: One of the parts that can be separated from crude oil.

Fractional distillation: The process of distilling crude oil in order to obtain useful products.

Fuel: Material that is burned to release its energy.

Gas: A material in which the particles are spread out from each other.

Global warming: The gradual increase in surface temperature of the Earth.

Greenhouse gases: They reduce the amount of energy lost from the Earth through radiation and therefore cause the temperature of the atmosphere to increase.

Hydrochloric acid: An acid which, when reacted with metals, produces salts called chlorides, such as sodium chloride and magnesium chloride.

Hydrogen: A highly flammable gas.

Incineration: A process of burning rubbish. It can be useful for getting rid of waste material, but can often produce toxic gases or greenhouse gases.

Iron: A metallic element not found in its natural state, but which has to be extracted from a compound in its ore.

Kinetic theory: A theory that says that all material is made up of tiny particles. These particles move:

- in solids, the particles vibrate but do not change place
- in liquids, the particles move with more energy and can change places
- in gases, the particles move at high speed.

Landfill sites: Sites where waste material can be buried in the ground; they are often used to dispose of household rubbish.

Limewater: A substance that turns cloudy if carbon dioxide is bubbled through it.

Liquid: A material in which the particles are closely packed but not in any definite or fixed pattern.

Low density: Low mass per unit volume.

Melting point: The temperature at which a substance changes from a solid to a liquid.

Metals: Shiny, good conductors of electricity and heat, malleable and ductile, and usually solid at room temperature.

Microbes: Microscopic organisms that are too small to be seen with the naked eye but can be seen under a microscope; microbes include bacteria, viruses and some fungi. Many microbes are very useful to us because they break down waste products.

Microorganism: Another name for a microbe.

Mixture: Two or more elements or compounds mixed together but not chemically bonded.

Moulded: When a material is pressed or squeezed into different shapes.

Neutralisation: Adding just the right amount of acid to an alkali so that the end product is neither acid nor alkaline.

Neutralise: To make the solution neither acid nor alkaline.

Non-metals: Dull, poor conductors of electricity and heat, brittle and usually solid or gaseous at room temperature.

Oil refinery: A processing plant where crude oil is separated out into useful products.

Oilfield: A place where there is enough oil to be found underground to make it worth extracting.

Ore: A rock with enough metal in it to make it worth extracting.

Oxidation: Reaction in which a substance combines with oxygen.

Periodic table: Shows all the elements arranged in rows and columns.

Photosynthesis: A process where plants and algae turn carbon dioxide and water into glucose and release oxygen.

Polythene: A common plastic which softens on heating and is unaffected by most chemicals.

Products: Substances formed in a chemical reaction, shown after the reaction arrow in an equation.

React: Chemical reactions occur when substances change to produce new substances.

Reactants: Substances that react together, shown before the arrow in an equation.

Reaction: A change in which a new substance is formed.

Recycle: Reuse materials.

Recycling: Processing a material so that it can be used again.

Rusting: Iron chemically combines with oxygen from the air to form a new substance called rust. Rusting happens very slowly and may take years to complete.

Salts: Substances produced when a metal and an acid react; common table salt is sodium chloride.

Solid: A material in which the particles are closely packed and usually in a regular pattern.

Solvent: A substance that dissolves another substance.

Soot: A form of carbon, usually a black powder.

Steels: Are alloys that always contain iron and carbon and sometimes other metals as well.

Sterilising: Means removing or killing bacteria and other microbes.

Strength: Materials with a high mechanical strength can withstand large forces without breaking.

Sulfuric acid: An acid which, when reacted with metals, produces salts called sulfates, such as copper sulfate and iron sulfate.

Unreactive: Does not chemically react with anything including air and water.

Word equation: A chemical word equation shows on the left-hand side those chemicals that reacted together (the reactants) and on the right-hand side the new chemicals that were made in the reaction (the products).

Physics

Absorber: An object that is taking in energy.

Air resistance: When an object moves through the air, there is friction between the object and the air, this can make a moving object slow down; streamlining helps to reduce air resistance.

Alpha particle: A particle given out from the nucleus of a radioactive atom. Alpha particles do not penetrate as much as beta particles or gamma rays.

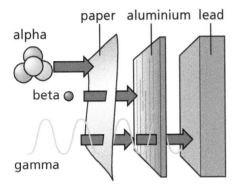

Alternating current: Continually changes direction very rapidly, flowing first one way and then the other.

Amplitude: The maximum amount of vibration, measured from the middle position of the wave, in metres.

Appliance: A piece of electrical equipment designed for a specific task, such as a radio.

Attraction: A pulling force.

Battery: A number of cells joined together.

Beta particle: A type of particle given out by a radioactive atom.

Braking distance: The distance travelled between the time at which the brakes are first applied and the time when the vehicle comes to a stop.

Braking force: The force that the driver applies to the brakes.

Cell: A cell pushes the electric current from the positive terminal round to the negative one.

Chemical energy: Emptied during chemical reactions when energy is transferred to the surroundings.

Component: Part of an electrical circuit, such as a lightbulb or battery.

Compression: Force squashing or pushing together.

Conductivity (heat): How well an object can transfer thermal energy.

Current: Flow of electric charge, measured in amperes (A).

Direct current: Always flows in the same direction.

Dissipated: Become spread out wastefully.

Earth wire: A wire connecting the metal case of an appliance to the ground.

Efficiency: A measure of how much of the input energy is changed into a useful form at the output.

Elastic potential energy: Filled when a material is stretched or compressed.

Electromagnet: A non-permanent magnet turned on and off by controlling the current through it.

Electromagnetic waves: A group of waves that possess many similar properties They are all capable of carrying energy.

Electrostatic force: Non-contact force between two charged objects.

Emit: To give out.

Emitter: An object that is giving out energy.

Energy: Energy is what allows us to do work, such as when moving things.

Energy resource: Something with stored energy that can be released in a useful way.

Energy store: There are many different types of energy store, including chemical, elastic, gravitational potential, kinetic and thermal.

Flex: A flexible electric wire.

Force: A push or a pull; it is measured in units called newtons (N).

Fossil fuels: Remains of dead organisms that are burned as fuels, releasing carbon dioxide.

Frequency: The number of waves produced in one second, in hertz (Hz).

Friction: Force opposing motion, caused by the interaction of surfaces moving over one another; it is called 'drag' if one surface is a fluid.

Fuse: A thin piece of wire designed to melt if the current becomes too large.

Gamma ray: A type of wave that carries a large amount of energy, given out by radioactive atoms. Gamma rays have extremely short wavelength and very penetrating waves; they can be produced during some types of radioactive decay.

Generator: A mechanical device that transfers kinetic energy (energy of movement) to produce electricity.

Geothermal energy: Energy that is provided by hot rocks beneath the surface of the ground.

Gravitational force: The force caused by the pull of the Earth.

Gravitational potential: Filled when an object is raised.

Hydroelectric: A way of producing electricity by allowing water from a high reservoir to run downhill and drive a turbine linked to a generator.

Infrared: The energy of these waves is often used for heating.

Insulation: A material that is not good at allowing thermal energy to be conducted through it.

Insulation: Plastic covering for an electrical wire that does not conduct electricity.

Ionising radiation: Radiation that can cause damage to living cells.

Kinetic energy: When an object moves.

Live wire: A wire that carries the current from the electricity generator to the appliance.

Longitudinal: Where the direction of vibration is the same as that of the wave.

Lubrication: A method of reducing friction, for example by adding lubricating oil.

Magnetic field: The space around a magnet in which a magnetic force exists.

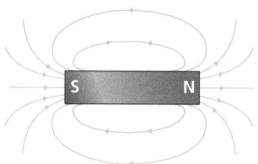

Magnetic force: Non-contact force from a magnet on a magnetic material.

Matt: Dull, not shiny.

Microwave: Some types of microwave are used in microwave cookers, others are used for communication, such as mobile phones or radar.

Neutral wire: A wire that returns the current from the appliance to the electricity generator.

Nuclear reactor: Part of a power station that uses radioactive materials as the energy source.

Nucleus: The centre part of an atom, which contains protons and neutrons.

Optical fibre: A very thin strand of glass, visible light and infrared waves can be sent along this fibre; the fibre acts rather like a pipe, carrying the waves inside.

Oscillation: A type of vibration, backwards and forwards or up and down.

Penetration: The ability of radiation to travel through different substances.

Perpendicular: At right angles to.

Poles: The ends of a magnetic field, called north-seeking (N) and south-seeking poles (S).

Power: How quickly energy is transferred by a device.

Power station: A place in which an energy resource is used to produce electricity, usually for the mains electricity supply.

Radar: A method used to detect aircraft and ships by reflecting electromagnetic waves from them.

Radiation: Transfer of thermal energy as a wave.

Radio: A means of communicating sound messages by converting them first into electromagnetic waves.

Radioactive: A material that can emit very high energy radiation.

Radioactivity: Some atoms are unstable and will break down, giving out alpha, beta or gamma radiation.

Range: How far radiation can travel before losing all of its energy.

Rarefaction: Stretched apart.

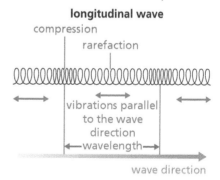

Reaction: A response made by the body to a stimulus.

Reaction time: The time between the body detecting a stimulus and producing a response.

Reflection: A change of direction of a wave when it meets a surface.

Relay: An electromagnet used to switch on or off another electrical circuit.

Renewable: An energy resource that can be replaced and will not run out; examples are solar, wind, waves, geothermal and biomass.

Repulsion: A pushing force.

Resistance: A property of a component, making it difficult for charge to pass through it; it is measured in ohms (Ω).

Satellite: A man-made object that can orbit the Earth.

Shiny: Polished, with a reflective surface.

Solar cell: A device that can use energy carried by light to produce electricity.

Solenoid: Wire wound into a tight coil, part of an electromagnet.

Spectrum: The whole band of electromagnetic waves.

Stopping distance: The total distance travelled between the driver first noticing the need to stop and the vehicle finally coming to a stop. The stopping distance is the thinking distance + braking distance.

| Thinking distance: the distance travelled during the driver's reaction time | Braking distance: the distance the car travels once the brakes have been pressed |

Thermal energy: Filled when an object is warmed up.

Thermostat: A device that controls the temperature in a room.

Thinking distance: The distance travelled between the driver first noticing the need to stop and the driver applying the brakes.

Transverse: Where the direction of vibration is perpendicular to that of the wave.

Tread: The tread on the surface of a tyre is the pattern of grooves that are cut into it; these grooves are designed to get rid of water from between the tyre and the road.

Turbine: A system of blades on an axle (like a propeller) that can be made to turn by air, steam or water being made to flow onto them.

Ultraviolet: Waves with frequencies higher than light, which human eyes cannot detect.

Vacuum: A space with no particles of matter in it.

Visible light: The waves that we can detect with our eyes.

Voltage: A measure of the size of the 'push' that is given to the electrons that form the current; the bigger the voltage, the bigger the current for any given resistance.

Wavelength: Distance between two corresponding points on a wave, in metres.

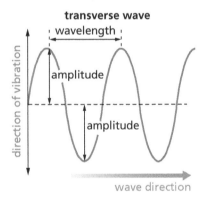

Work: The transfer of energy when a force moves an object, measured in joules (J).

X-rays: Very short wavelength waves that can pass through many substances that visible light cannot.

Outcome 1: Cells

1. *From the top*: cytoplasm [1]; nucleus [1]; cell membrane [1]

2. Nucleus – contains genetic information, which controls the activities of the cell [1]; Cytoplasm – where chemical reactions happen [1]; Cell membrane – controls what enters and leaves the cell [1]

3. nerve [1]; egg [1]; muscle [1]

4. **a** sperm (cell) [1]

   b So it can swim [1] and reach the egg/female sex cell [1]

Outcome 2: Tissues, organs and systems

1. cell – tissue – organ [1]

2. Brain – receives and processes information [1]; Kidney – filters the blood and produces urine (a liquid waste) [1]; Liver – does many jobs, including removing toxins from the blood [1]

3. testes [1]; ovaries [1]

4. 2 – Blood is pumped around the body [1]; 3 – Blood high in carbon dioxide returns to the heart and is pumped to the lungs [1]; 4 – In the lungs carbon dioxide leaves the blood and oxygen enters it [1]

5. Cell X: Name: red blood cell [1]; Function: carry oxygen around to all parts of the body [1]

   Cell Y: Name: white blood cell [1]; Function: help to fight diseases [1]

Outcome 3: The digestive system

1. *From the top*: oesophagus [1]; stomach [1]; pancreas [1]; large intestine [1]

2. stomach [1]; small intestine [1]

3. The process of breaking down food into simple substances that the blood can absorb. [1]

4. stomach [1]; pancreas [1]; small intestine [1]

5. **a** The mixture would not go black *or* The mixture would go orange when starch is added. [1]

   b decrease [1]; There is more amylase to break down the starch. [1]

Outcome 4: Respiration and lifestyle

1. **a** oxygen [1]; water [1]

   b food *or* diet [1]

   c lungs [1]

2. Smoking – lung cancer [1]; Drinking too much alcohol – liver and brain damage [1]

3. Their pulse rate went up. [1]

4. **a** Isabel [1]

   b After exercise Isabel's pulse rate returned to resting rate more quickly than Briony's pulse. [1]

Outcome 5: Pathogens

1. Can spread/pass between people [1]

2. cancer [1]

3. reproduce [1]; toxins [1]

4. **a** 37 (°C) [1]

   b It increased/went up [1]

5. **a** Bacteria that cause disease produce toxins [1] that make us feel ill. [1]

   b They damage cells [1] by living/reproducing inside them [1]

Outcome 6: Fighting disease

1. antibodies [1]

2. **a** *From the top*: bacteria [1]; white blood cell [1]

   b It ingests/consumes them [1]

3. **a** an inactive virus [1]

   b 1 – White blood cells start to produce antibodies to fight the virus. [1] 2 – The white blood cells remember how to make the antibodies for the measles virus. [1] 3 – If Connor becomes infected with active measles viruses his body will quickly produce antibodies. [1]

   c The viruses are dead/inactive. [1]

   d The antibodies have remembered how to make antibodies against the measles virus [1]; so produce them quickly to destroy the viruses. [1]

4. **a** It decreased [1]

   b People who had the injection did not get measles. [1]

Outcome 7: Drugs

1. alcohol [1]
2. **a** penicillin [1]
   b Antibiotics only kill bacteria. [1]
3. addictive [1]; withdrawal [1]
4. To check that the medicine is safe [1]; to check that the medicine works. [1]
5. antibiotic 1 [1]; the area where the bacteria have died is larger (than antibiotic 2). [1]

Outcome 8: Control systems

1. brain [1]; nerve cells [1]
2. Pulling your hand away when you touch a hot pan [1]; the pupil of your eye getting smaller in bright light. [1]
3. fast [1]; automatic [1]
4. **a** 0.22 [1]
   b He drinks some coffee and repeats the investigation [1]. Compare his reaction times to the previous results to see if they are quicker. [1]

Outcome 9: Hormones

1. gland [1]; liver [1]; blood [1]
2. **a** 28 [1]
   b 1 [1]
3. **a** 14 [1]; 21 [1]
   b oestrogen [1]; it is highest on the day in the menstrual cycle that an egg is released [1]
4. day 11–18 [1]

Outcome 10: Controlling fertility

1. She does not release any eggs [1]; her eggs do not mature. [1]
2. pill [1]; inhibit [1]
3. **a** They are 99% effective at preventing pregnancy. [1]
   b The woman might forget to take it. [1]
4. **a** They cause more eggs to mature and be released [1]; so there is a higher chance that an egg will meet a sperm. [1]
   b It could cause a multiple pregnancy [1]; risk of complications in pregnancy/birth *or* risk of premature babies. [1]

1. oxygen [1]
2. **a** tissues [1]; organs [1]
   b Circulatory system – transports oxygen and other substances around the body [1]; Reproductive system – produces offspring [1]; Digestive system – breaks down food into soluble substances that can enter the blood [1]
   c Digestive [1]
3. **a** Infectious [1]; microorganisms [1]
   b Viruses [1]
4. **a** cancer [1]
   b Your body becomes dependent on *or* Once you start taking it, you want more *or* It is difficult to give up. [1]
5. white blood cells [1]
6. **a** it gets smaller [1]
   b reflex [1]
7. **a** Nucleus [1]
   b Controls the movement of substances in and out of cells [1]
8. **a** glands [1]; blood [1]
   b They stimulate eggs to mature [1]

Component 2 – Biology: Environment, evolution and inheritance

Outcome 1: Feeding relationships

1. oak tree [1]; algae [1]
2. **a** Substances that are used in photosynthesis – carbon dioxide [1]; water [1]
   Substances that are made in photosynthesis – oxygen [1]; glucose [1]
   b light [1]; chlorophyll [1]
3. **a** Points plotted correctly. [2] (1 mark if only two points plotted correctly)
   b Curved line drawn through the points. [1]
   c decreased [1]; light [1]
4. Plants need light to make their food [1]; animals eat plants. [1]

Outcome 2: Adaptation

1. a habitat [1]; adapted [1]

  b *Any one from:* water stored in leaves/stem; long roots to absorb water; spikes to reduce water loss [1]

2. White fur – for camouflage [1]; Thick fur – to keep warm [1]; Sharp claws – to kill prey [1]

3. a 52 – 26 = 26 (°C) [1]

  b The results show that the water in the beaker with the fur cooled down more slowly than the water in the beaker without the fur [1]. Polar bears have fur because it slows down heat loss. [1]

Outcome 3: Food chains and webs

1. a grass [1]; owl [1]

  b An animal that eats other animals. [1]

  c shrew [1]

2. a owls [1]; foxes [1]

  b Nothing eats them *or* they don't have predators. [1]

  c It increases [1]

3. Rabbits also have grass to eat. [1]

Outcome 4: Recycling materials

1. die [1]; microorganisms [1]

2. warm and damp [1]

3. a photosynthesis [1]

  b *Any one from*: respiration *or* burning wood and fossil fuels [1]

  c Feeding/eating [1]

4. Leave grapes in different temperatures for a period of time [1]; see which grape has broken down the most [1] *or* leave grapes at different temperatures [1]; measure how long it takes for the grape to break down at each temperature. [1]

Outcome 5: Competition

1. food [1]; mates [1]

2. a Both lion and cheetahs eat antelopes. [1]

  b true [1]

3. compete [1]; water [1]

4. light [1]

5. a *Any one from:* food/space/territory [1]

  b The grey squirrels are bigger than the red squirrels so get the resources [1] and so red squirrels do not have enough resources and die. [1]

Outcome 6: Abiotic and biotic factors

1. Environment – the surroundings that an organism lives in [1]; Abiotic factor – a non-living factor of an ecosystem [1[; Biotic factor – a living factor of an ecosystem [1]

2. temperature [1]; soil type [1]

3. a temperature [1]; increased [1]

  b extinct [1]

4. It will be lower at point Y [1] because the tree reduces the amount of light reaching the ground [1] *or* it is in the shade of the tree. [1]

5. It will increase [1]; because there are no foxes to eat them. [1]

Outcome 7: Pollution

1. sulfur dioxide [1]; smoke [1]

2. smoke [1]; sulfur [1]

3. Sewage – waste material that contains faeces and urine [1]; herbicide – a toxic chemical used to kill weeds [1]; Pesticide – a toxic substance used to kill pests [1]

4. a deforestation [1]

  b *Any sensible answer e.g.* to use the trees for wood/to make space for building houses/farming/roads/quarrying [1]

5. a less dirt [1]

  b There is less pollution from the cars further from the road. [1]

Outcome 8: Evolution

1. natural [1]; Darwin [1]; simple [1]

2. a fossils [1]

  b increased height [1]; decreased number of toes [1]

3. a selective *or* artificial [1]

  b Breed from the fastest dogs. [1]

4. a The dark moths are not camouflaged [1] so will be eaten by birds. [1]

  b The number of pale moths will go down [1]; the number of dark moths will go up. [1]

  c natural [1]

Outcome 9: Reproduction

1. egg [1]; sperm [1]
2. genetic [1]; offspring [1]
3. The new plant has the same characteristics as the parent plant. [1]
4. **a** asexual [1]

   b quicker [1]
5. They have two f/white fur versions of the gene [1], one from each parent. [1]

Outcome 10: DNA, genes and chromosomes

1. *From top:* nucleus [1]; chromosome [1]; DNA [1]; gene [1]
2. 46 [1]
3. same [1]; XY [1]
4. 2 – The insulin gene is cut out. [1]; 3 – The insulin gene is inserted into the bacteria's DNA. [1]; 4 – The bacteria reproduces many times and produces insulin. [1]
5. We do not know the long term risks *or* possibility of genes transferring to wild plants *or* possible danger to human health when eating them. [1]
6. Taller people have larger arm spans. [1]

Mini test answers

1. **a** algae → turtles → alligators[1]

   b algae [1]
2. water [1]; oxygen [1]
3. **a** light [1]

   b insects that eat plants
4. **a** There is a mixing of genetic information, which leads to variety in the offspring. [1]

   b sexual [1]

   c sperm [1]
5. **a** The slow cheetahs will not get enough food. [1]

   b genes [1]; offspring [1]

   c (Charles) Darwin [1]
6. Cactus – can store water [1]; Polar bear – thick layer of fat for warmth [1]; Shark – gills for breathing [1]
7. **a** 45 + 18 = 63 (million) [1]

   b Toxic chemicals that pollute the land. [1]
8. microorganisms [1]; photosynthesis [1]

Component 3 – Chemistry: Elements, mixtures and compounds

Outcome 1: Atoms and elements

1. The smallest part of an element that can exist. [1]
2. 100 [1]; Rb [1]; Cl [1]
3. Shiny – Metals [1]; Low boiling point – Non-metals [1]; Good conductor of heat – Metals [1]; Poor conductor of electricity – Non-metals [1]
4. *Two from:* it has properties of metals and non-metals [1]; it does not conduct heat easily [1]; it has low strength [1]

Outcome 2: Making compounds

1. Compounds are made of elements. [1]
2. B and D [1]
3. a compound [1]
4. Carbon dioxide – non-metals combined [1]; Sodium chloride – metal and non-metal combined [1]; Iron oxide – metal and non-metal combined [1]
5. Oxygen – Reactant [1]; Magnesium – Reactant [1]; Magnesium oxide – Product [1]
6. sulfur + oxygen *or* oxygen + sulfur [1]
7. **a** iron + chlorine → iron chloride [1]

   b carbon + oxygen → carbon dioxide [1]

Outcome 3: States of matter

1. solid – bottom diagram [1]; liquid – middle diagram [1]; gas – top diagram [1]
2. melts [1]; condenses [1]
3. It can condense or boil. [1]
4. Particles are close together – Solid [1] *and* Liquid [1]; Particles are in fixed positions – Solid [1]; Particles can move about at high speed – Gas [1]
5. They move far apart and begin to move around rapidly. [1]
6. Arrangement: the particles stay close together. [1]; Movement: the particles start to move *or* begin to change places. [1]

Outcome 4: Diamond and graphite

1. Soft – Graphite [1]; Hard – Diamond [1]; Slippery – Graphite [1]
2. Labels are (*clockwise from the top right*): strong bond [1]; graphite [1]; diamond [1]; carbon atom [1]

3. carbon [1]; giant [1]; layers [1]

4. a It is very hard. [1]

 b jewellery [1]

5. It has layers that can slide over each other. [1]

6. Graphite has layers [1] but diamond does not [1]; *or* Atoms are joined to four atoms in diamond [1] but are joined to three atoms in graphite. [1]

Outcome 5: Separating mixtures

1. B [1]

2. Mixtures can be solids, liquids or gases. [1]

3. Air – Mixture [1]; Gold – Pure substance [1]; Seawater – Mixture [1]

4. top diagram – chromatography [1]; bottom diagram – filtration [1]

5. crystallisation [1]; distillation [1]; filtration [1]; chromatography [1]

6. filtration [1]; (*then*) crystallisation [1]

Outcome 6: Paper chromatography

1. A mixture of food dyes for a cake. [1]

2. Labels are (*top to bottom*): test tube [1]; paper [1]; sample spot [1]; solvent [1]

3. Correct order is (after 1): 3, 5, 2, 4; *all correct* [3] *2 correct* [2] *1 correct* [1]

4. a B [1]

 b C [1]

 c A and C *or* C and A [1]

5. a Pencil does not dissolve in the solvent *or* pen ink would dissolve in the solvent. [1]

 b So the substances do not leave the paper *or* dissolve into the solvent at the bottom. [1]

Outcome 7: Extracting metals

1. economic [1]

2. a iron *or* copper *or* gold [1]

 b magnesium *or* calcium [1]

 c iron [1]

3. It is unreactive. [1]

4. Correct order is: 1 – Mine large amounts of rocks that contain zinc ore; 2 – Separate the zinc ore from the rocks; 3 – Heat the zinc ore with carbon; 4 – Purify the zinc. *All correct* [3] *2 correct* [2] *1 correct* [1]

5. To reduce the need to quarry ores. [1]

6. *Two from the following for one mark each*: habitats destroyed [1]; noisy [1]; dusty [1]; uses up finite resources [1]; a lot of waste produced [1]; extra traffic from the mine [1]; damage because of energy needed, e.g. pollution from burning fuels, drilling for oil [1]

Outcome 8: Metals

1. Four circles drawn, similar size to the ones shown [1]; regular arrangement and touching [1]

2. There are strong bonds between atoms. [1]

3. sodium [1]

4. corrosion [1]

5. Conducts electricity easily and easily bent – electrical wiring [1]; Low density and resists corrosion – aircraft parts [1]

6. copper [1]

7. *Two from*: good electrical conductor [1]; low density *or* light weight [1]; resists corrosion [1]; strong [1]

Outcome 9: Alloys

1. a To make the metal harder. [1]

 b alloy [1]

 c 5% [1]

2. 40% [1]

3. Iron mixed with carbon and other metals. [1]

4. Pure iron is too soft *or* steels are harder than pure iron [1]; steels have more uses than pure iron [1]

Outcome 10: Polymers

1. a Ethene is a monomer and (poly)ethene is a polymer. [1]

 b Not affected by acids and alkalis. [1]

2. a heated [1]

 b rolled [1]

 c moulded [1]

3. A substance that is broken down by microbes. [1]

4. Incineration – burning waste at high temperatures [1]; Landfill site – place where waste can be buried underground [1]

5. There are different types of polymer [1]; they have to be sorted *or* different polymers have to be separated *or* they have to be recycled differently [1]

169

1. **a** Glass from a mixture of glass and water – filtration [1]; Pure water from ink – distillation [1]

   b distances [1]

2. **a** solid [1]

   b alloy [1]

   c harder [1]; corrosion [1]

3. **a** It is made of only one sort of atom. [1]

   b Most of them are metals. [1]

   c Li and Na [1]

   d carbon + oxygen *or* oxygen + carbon [1]

4. **a** waterproof [1]

   b recycle [1]; biodegradable [1]

5. **a** carbon [1]

   b Hard – diamond [1]; Slippery – graphite [1]; Atoms arranged in layers – graphite [1]

6. **a** It is a compound. [1]

   b Zinc [1]

Component 4 – Chemistry: Chemistry in our world

Outcome 1: Acids and salts

1. Hydrochloric acid – iron chloride [1]; Sulfuric acid– iron sulfate [1]

2. (zinc) chloride [1]; hydrogen [1]

3. **a** (burning) splint/spill [1]

   b hydrogen [1]

   c It will burn with a squeaky pop sound. [1]

   d magnesium chloride [1]

4. **a** Same volume of acid [1]; Same concentration of acid. [1]

   b type of metal [1]

Outcome 2: Neutralisation

1. Acid – hydrochloric acid [1]; Alkali – potassium hydroxide [1]; Insoluble base – Magnesium oxide [1]

2. sodium hydroxide, water [2]; sulfuric acid [1]; zinc sulfate, carbon dioxide [2]

3. crystals [1]; solution [1]; crystallisation [1]

4. **a** carbon dioxide [1]

   b chloride [1]; carbon dioxide [1]

c carbon dioxide [1]; milky/white/cloudy [1]

d No visible reaction. [1]

Outcome 3: Energy transfers in chemistry

1. B [1]; A [1]; B [1]; C [1]

2. A – in [1]; B – out [1]; C – out [1]; D – in [1]

3. **a** 12 [1]; 19 [1]

   b Bars drawn the same width as the zinc oxide bar [1]; iron oxide bar drawn up to 12 °C [1]; magnesium oxide bar drawn up to 19 °C [1]

   c Type of the metal oxide. [1]

Outcome 4: Rate of reaction

1. Increase the temperature of the hydrochloric acid [1]; Use more concentrated hydrochloric acid [1]; Use magnesium powder instead of magnesium strip. [1]

2. **a** 40 [1]; 50 [1]

   b The length of magnesium strip was the same in both experiments. [1]

   c 50 °C [1]

   d the line is steeper [1]

Outcome 5: The early atmosphere

1. **a** carbon dioxide [1]

   b volcanoes [1]

   c atmosphere [1]; water vapour [1]; condensed [1]

2. **a** plants and algae [1]

   b photosynthesis [1]

   c carbon dioxide + water → glucose + oxygen [1]

3. The atmosphere of Mars contains a similar percentage of carbon dioxide as the early atmosphere of Earth. [1]

Outcome 6: The atmosphere today

1. carbon dioxide [1]; photosynthesis [1]; dissolved [1]; oceans [1]

2. One large sector of 8 segments [1]; one smaller sector of 2 segments [1]; correctly labelled. [1]

3. It has been converted into coal, oil and gas [1]; It has been converted into carbonate rocks. [1]

4. **a** 16 [1]

   b Respiration uses up oxygen and releases carbon dioxide. [1]

   c nitrogen [1]

Outcome 7: Crude oil

1. mixture [1]

2. fractions [1]; refinery [1]; useful [1]; petrol [1]

3. a fractional distillation [1]

   b petrol [1]; diesel [1]

   c aircraft fuel [1] (*also accept* heating buildings [1])

4. a (refinery) gas [1]

   b The temperature is high at the bottom of the column [1] and decreases further up the column. [1]

Outcome 8: Burning fuels

1. complete [1]; fuel [1]; oxygen [1]; combustion [1]; limited [1]

2. carbon dioxide [1]; water vapour [1]; sulfur dioxide [1]

3. Carbon monoxide is produced, which is a poisonous gas. [1]

4. Sulfur dioxide – acid rain [1]; Solid soot particles – global dimming [1]

5. It is colourless *or* we cannot see it [1]; it is odourless *or* we cannot smell it. [1]

6. *Any two of*: reduces acid rain; reduces global warming; reduces global dimming [2]

Outcome 9: Greenhouse gases

1. methane [1]; carbon dioxide [1]

2. cattle farming [1]; burning coal [1]; putting food waste in landfill [1]

3. a Many scientists agree about the link [1]; Some scientists do not agree about the link. [1]

   b rising sea levels [1]; greater risk of droughts [1]

4. stayed about the same [1]; increased [1]; increased [1]

Outcome 10: Water for drinking

1. small [1]; dissolved [1]; microbes [1]

2. filtering *or* filtration [1]

3. to kill microbes [1]

4. lakes [1]; rivers [1]

5. a Bunsen burner *or* electrical (retort) heater [1]

   b distillation [1]

   c The process uses a lot of energy. [1]

1. a nitrogen [1]

   b photosynthesis by plants and algae [1]

   c locked [1]; carbonate [1]

2. a neutralisation [1]

   b sulfuric acid + potassium hydroxide → potassium sulfate + water [1]

   c A burning splint burns quickly with a squeaky pop sound. [1]

3. a filtration [1]

   b The fresh water needs to be sterilised to kill any microbes. [1]

4. a mixture [1]; fractions [1]

   b fractional distillation [1]

   c Acid rain – sulfur dioxide [1] Global warming – carbon dioxide [1]

5. increases [1]; decreases [1]

6. a Measuring the time taken to produce 10 cm³ samples of the carbon dioxide gas. [1]

   Measuring the time taken for the white compound to completely disappear. [1]

   b *Any two of*: increasing the temperature *or* increasing the concentration of the acid *or* increasing the surface area of the calcium carbonate *or* adding a catalyst. [2]

Component 5 – Physics: Energy, forces and the structure of matter

Outcome 1: Energy changes

1. The kettle's store of thermal energy increases. [1]

2. An apple hanging in a tree – gravitational potential [1]; An apple that has been thrown – kinetic [1]; An apple in the oven – thermal [1]

3. down [1]; up [1]; up [1]

4. The brakes have more thermal energy. [1]

5. elastic [1]; kinetic [1]; gravitational potential [1]

Outcome 2: Energy transfers

1. Absorber – an object that is taking in energy [1]; Emitter – an object that is giving out energy [1]; Radiation – transfer of thermal energy as a wave [1]

2. more efficient [1]

3. **a** Light-coloured walls reflect more radiation. [1]

   b insulators [1]; lower [1]; decrease [1]

4. There is no air in the gap of the flask, to reduce heat conduction [1]; The walls of the flask are polished and shiny, to reflect the radiation. [1]

Outcome 3: Energy resources

1. Bio-fuels are a renewable energy resource. [1]

2. oil power stations [1]; nuclear power stations [1]

3. turbine [1]; generator [1]

4. disadvantage [1]; advantage [1]; advantage [1]

5. The turbine blades in the water spin around – 2 [1]; This turns an electrical generator – 3 [1]; Electricity is then taken back to shore by cables on the sea floor – 4 [1]

Outcome 4: Contact and non-contact forces

1. gravitational [1]

2. *up*: normal contact force [1]; *down*: weight [1]

3. force [1]; friction [1]

4. air resistance [1]

5. An electron moving around the nucleus – electrostatic [1]; A conker spinning around on a string – tension [1]; The Earth orbiting the sun – gravitational [1]

Outcome 5: Work

1. The friction between the hands heats them up. [1]

2. Work – how much energy is transferred when a force moves an object, measured in joules [1]; Force – a push or a pull, measured in newtons [1]; Friction – a contact force that tries to slow down a moving object [1]

3. pushing force [1]; work done [1]

4. So that they are cooled by the air passing them. [1]

5. work [1]; weight [1]; 3000 joules [1]

Outcome 6: Speed

1. 96 kilometres per hour [1]

2. $\dfrac{180}{3}$ [1] = 60 miles per hour [2]

3. Oscar [1]

4. **a** Zoe [1]

   b Yumi [1]

5. $\dfrac{200}{50}$ = 4 m/s; [1]; $\dfrac{500}{100}$ = 5 m/s [1]; 1 m/s [1]

Outcome 7: Stopping distances

1. both [1]

2. **a** 9 m + 14 m = 23 m [1]

   b four times [1]

3. **a** does not change [1]

   b decreases [1]

4. 24 m [1]; 53 m [1]; 21 m [1]

Outcome 8: Reaction times

1. 21 cm [1]

2. increased [1]

3. It increases reaction times [1]; Drunk drivers make worse decisions [1]

4. sometimes [1]; slower [1]

5. Rosa is tired [1]; Rosa has been drinking alcohol [1]; There are young children in the back being silly. [1]

Outcome 9: Braking distance

1. **a** dry road [1]

   b increases [1]

2. **a** thinking distance [1]; braking distance [1]

   b stopping distance [1]

3. Its brakes are bigger and stronger [1]; The tyres are wider, resulting in better grip. [1]

4. The treads are needed to push the water out from under the tyre [1]; If the treads are not deep enough the car will have a bigger stopping or braking distance. [1]

Outcome 10: Atoms and nuclear radiation

1. nucleus [1]

2. *From top to bottom*: alpha particle [1]; gamma ray [1]

3. Alpha particles are stopped by 1–2 cm of air *or* alpha particles cannot reach you. [1]

4. Alpha particles – smoke detectors [1]; Beta particles – measuring the thickness of aluminium foil [1]; Gamma rays – sterilising medical equipment [1]

5. alpha – not detected [1]; beta – detected [1]; gamma – detected [1]

1. more [1]; the same [1]

2. Insulation reduces your heat loss [1] (so less energy is needed)

3. coal power stations [1]; oil power stations [1]

4. air resistance [1]; friction [1]; tension [1]

5. goes down [1]; goes down [1]; friction [1]

6. $\frac{60}{2}$ = 30 kilometres per hour [1]

7. Braking distance – the distance the car travels once the brakes have been pressed [1]; Stopping distance – the distance a car travels from when the driver sees an event to when it comes to a stop [1]; Thinking distance – the distance the car travels during the driver's reaction time [1]

8. a Quinn drops the ruler and Romeo catches it as quickly as he can, and they record the distance it fell. [1]

   b The further the ruler travels the slower the reaction time. [1]

9. a leaves on the track [1]

   b There will also be a thinking distance *or* the train travels a certain distance before the driver can react. [1]

10. gamma rays [1]

Component 6 – Physics: Electricity, magnetism and waves

Outcome 1: Electric current

1. charge [1]

2. electrons [1]

3. battery [1]; circuit [1]; conductor [1]

4. Resistance – a measure of how difficult it is for an electric current to pass through a component [1]; Current – the flow of electric charge [1]

5. a ammeter [1]

   b voltmeter [1]

   c smaller [1]

Outcome 2: a.c. and d.c. current

1. direct current [1]

2. Alternating current – current that changes direction [1]; Frequency – alternating current changes direction and back again at 50 hertz (50 times per second) in the UK [1]; Voltage – alternating current is delivered to UK houses at 230 volts [1]

3. a d.c. moves in the same direction [1]

   b a.c. changes direction [1]

4. complete [1]; gaps [1]; direct [1]

5. The ring main has a voltage of 230 V [1]; The ring main is an alternating current. [1]

Outcome 3: Electrical appliances and safety

1. three-core flex [1]

2. *Clockwise from right*: live wire [1]; neutral wire [1]; earth wire [1]

3. a live wire [1]

   b B → C → A: *if 2 in sequence* [1]; *all 3 correct* [2]

4. plastic [1]; wire [1]; casing [1]

Outcome 4: Electrical appliances and energy transfer

1. The power of the appliance [1]

2. 1 kilowatt [1]; 1.2 kilowatts [1]; 0.02 kilowatts [1]

3. hours [1]

4. 2.15 × 0.5 = 1.075 (kWh) *for using 2.15 kW* [1]; *for using 0.5* [1]; *correct answer* [1]

Outcome 5: Magnets and magnetic fields

1. Like poles will repel each other. [1]

2. N------S N------S; *North pole on second magnet not required for mark* [1]

3. a attracting [1]; pulling [1]

   b repelling [1]; pushing [1]

4 non-contact force [1]

5. Symmetrical shape [1]; at least three field lines close together at poles – with arrows [1]; at least two field lines further apart at sides. [1] (*Arrows not required for mark*)

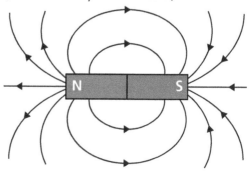

Outcome 6: Electromagnets

1. increases [1]; decreases [1] (*also accept* decreases [1]; increases [1])

2. **a** An iron core/nail has been inserted into the solenoid. [1]

   b Increase the current passing through the wire *or* increase the number of coils in the solenoid. [1]

3. current [1]; stronger [1]; magnetism [1]

4. The electromagnetic can be switched off so that the iron/steel (*accept metal*) can be dropped in the right place [1]; an ordinary magnet cannot be switched off so the metal would be stuck to it. [1]

Outcome 7: Transverse and longitudinal waves

1. **a** transverse [1]

   b longitudinal [1]

2. Transverse wave – oscillations are perpendicular (at right-angles) to the direction of energy transfer [1]; Longitudinal wave – oscillations are parallel to the direction of energy transfer [1]

3. particles [1]; closer together [1]; particles [1]; further apart [1]

Outcome 8: Wave characteristics

1. third waveform [1]

2. *Both vertical arrows*: amplitude [1]; *both horizontal arrows*: wavelength [1]

3. amplitude [1]

4. **a** Wave A [1]

   b A – 2 hertz [1]; B – 3 hertz [1]

5. **a** wavelength = 0.2 metres [1]

   b Wave speed = 1650 × 0.2 metres per second [1] = 330 metres per second [1]

Outcome 9: Electromagnetic waves

1. Ultraviolet waves – between visible light waves and X-rays [1]; X-rays – between ultraviolet waves and gamma rays [1]; Microwaves – between radio waves and infrared waves [1]

2. **a** infrared waves [1]

   b *Any one of*: infrared, microwaves or radio waves [1]

3. gamma rays [1]; radio waves [1]; X-rays [1]

4. **a** gamma rays [1]; X-rays [1]

   b The level of hazard due to these waves can be reduced by *any two from*: reducing the frequency [1]; reducing the amplitude (intensity) [1]; inserting a barrier (to absorb the radiation) [1]; reducing the time we are exposed to the radiation. [1]

Outcome 10: Uses of electromagnetic waves

1. fibre-optic communications [1]

2. Infrared waves – heating [1]; Microwaves – cooking food [1]; Light waves – desk lamp [1]

3. gamma rays [1]; ultraviolet waves [1]; X-rays [1]

4. **a** infrared waves [1]

   b infrared [1]; eyes [1]

Mini test answers

1. **a** current [1]

   b battery [1]

2. 230 volts [1]

3. **a** earth wire [1]

   b to carry the current [1]

   c fuse [1]

4. **a** 2 kW [1]

   b 0.1 kWh [1]

5. They strongly attract. [1]

6. **a** electromagnet *or* solenoid *or* coil [1]

   b The iron core will lose its magnetism when the circuit is broken *or* a permanent magnet will not lose its magnetism. [1]

7. **a** longitudinal wave [1]

   b transverse wave [1]

   c wavelength [1]

   d amplitude [1]

8. **a** microwaves [1]

   b ultraviolet waves [1]

9. Infrared waves – cooking food [1]; Visible light waves – fibre-optic communications [1]; X-rays – medical imaging of bones [1]